HISPANIC AMERICA, TEXAS, *and the* MEXICAN WAR

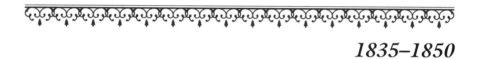

1835–1850

HISPANIC AMERICA, TEXAS, *and the* MEXICAN WAR

1835–1850

Christopher Collier
James Lincoln Collier

BENCHMARK BOOKS

MARSHALL CAVENDISH
NEW YORK

ACKNOWLEDGMENT: The authors wish to thank Howard R. Lamar, Sterling Professor Emeritus of History and former President, Yale University, and Arnoldo DeLeon, C. J. "Red" Davidson Professor of History, Angelo State University, for their careful reading of the text of this volume of The Drama of American History and their thoughtful and useful comments. The work has been much improved by their notes. The authors are deeply in their debt but, of course, assume full responsibility for the substance of the work, including any errors.

Photo research by James Lincoln Collier.
COVER PHOTO: Prints and Photographs Division, Library of Congress.
PICTURE CREDITS: The photographs in this book are used by permission and through the courtesy of:
Corbis-Bettmann: 11, 12 (top right), 14, 15, 25, 30 (top), 46 (bottom), 48, 50, 52, 53, 54, 61, 62, 75, 81, 83.
National Museum of the American Indian: 12 (top left), 12 (bottom), 26, 59 (top), 59 (bottom). Prints and Photographs Division, Library of Congress: 18, 30 (bottom), 35, 38, 67, 69, 73 (top), 73 (bottom), 76, 77.
Joslyn Art Museum: 40, 41.

Benchmark Books
Marshall Cavendish Corporation
99 White Plains Road
Tarrytown, New York 10591-9001

©1999 Christopher Collier and James Lincoln Collier

Library of Congress Cataloging-in-Publication Data

Collier, Christopher, date
Hispanic America, Texas and the Mexican War, 1835–1850 / Christopher Collier, James Lincoln Collier.
p. cm.   —(Drama of American history)
Includes bibliographical references and index.
Summary: Examines the settlement of the area that became the southwestern portion of the United States, detailing how it evolved from land settled by Native Americans, to Spanish territory, to states that were pawns between the North and South prior to the Civil War.
ISBN 0-7614-0780-4 (lib. bdg.)
1. Southwest, New—History—to 1848—Juvenile literature. 2. Mexican War, 1846–1848—Juvenile literature.
[1. Southwest, New—History—to 1848. 2. United States—Territorial expansion.]
I. Collier, James Lincoln, date. II. Title. III. Series: Collier, Christopher, date, Drama of American history.
F800.C64   1999
979'.02–dc21   97-34962
                                              CIP
                                              AC

Printed in Italy

1 3 5 6 4 2

CONTENTS

PREFACE   7

CHAPTER I   The Coming of the Europeans to the Southwest   9

CHAPTER II   The Creation of the Southwest Hispanic Culture 23

CHAPTER III   Manifest Destiny   34

CHAPTER IV   The War with Mexico   45

CHAPTER V   California, Here I Come   58

CHAPTER VI   California Compromise   71

BIBLIOGRAPHY   85

INDEX   89

Over many years of both teaching and writing for students at all levels, from grammar school to graduate school, it has been borne in on us that many, if not most, American history textbooks suffer from trying to include everything of any moment in the history of the nation. Students become lost in a swamp of factual information, and as a consequence lose track of how those facts fit together and why they are significant and relevant to the world today.

In this series, our effort has been to strip the vast amount of available detail down to a central core. Our aim is to draw in bold strokes, providing enough information, but no more than is necessary, to bring out the basic themes of the American story, and what they mean to us now. We believe that it is surely more important for students to grasp the underlying concepts and ideas that emerge from the movement of history, than to memorize an array of facts and figures.

The difference between this series and many standard texts lies in what has been left out. We are convinced that students will better remember the important themes if they are not buried under a heap of names, dates, and places.

In this sense, our primary goal is what might be called citizenship education. We think it is critically important for America as a nation and Americans as individuals to understand the origins and workings of the public institutions that are central to American society. We have asked ourselves again and again what is most important for citizens of our democracy to know so they can most effectively make the system work for them and the nation. For this reason, we have focused on political and institutional history, leaving social and cultural history less well developed.

This series is divided into volumes that move chronologically through the American story. Each is built around a single topic, such as the Pilgrims, the Constitutional Convention, or immigration. Each volume has been written so that it can stand alone, for students who wish to research a given topic. As a consequence, in many cases material from previous volumes is repeated, usually in abbreviated form, to set the topic in its historical context. That is to say, students of the Constitutional Convention must be given some idea of relations with England, and why the Revolution was fought, even though the material was covered in detail in a previous volume. Readers should find that each volume tells an entire story that can be read with or without reference to other volumes.

Despite our belief that it is of the first importance to outline sharply basic concepts and generalizations, we have not neglected the great dramas of American history. The stories that will hold the attention of students are here, and we believe they will help the concepts they illustrate to stick in their minds. We think, for example, that knowing of Abraham Baldwin's brave and dramatic decision to vote with the small states at the Constitutional Convention will bring alive the Connecticut Compromise, out of which grew the American Senate.

Each of these volumes has been read by esteemed specialists in its particular topic; we have benefited from their comments.

CHAPTER I

The Coming of the Europeans to the Southwest

The southwestern section of the United States, including the present states of Texas, Arizona, New Mexico, California, and parts of Nevada and Utah, has a history that is somewhat different from the rest of the nation. Most of the rest of the nation was settled by English people and their descendants, beginning in Jamestown in 1607 and Plymouth in 1620. From these first tiny settlements, these English-speaking people with English ways pushed westward, at first slowly, and then in a rush, until they occupied most of the land from the Atlantic to the Pacific. (For the story of the first English settlers see *The Paradox of Jamestown* and *Pilgrims and Puritans,* the second and third volumes in this series). People from other countries and ethnic groups did of course come to North America—at first Irish and Germans, and then others from almost every national group elsewhere. Nonetheless, the English settled the area that later became the United States first, and American ways are still basically derived from the English ones that the first settlers brought with them, although of course they have been modified by the cultures of later arrivals.

But the first European settlers in the huge southwestern corner of the modern United States were Spanish, and a strong Hispanic influence remains in this part of the United States today.

The story of the Spanish conquest of Mexico, Central America and much of South America is fascinating, and much too large for this book. To describe it briefly, once Columbus discovered the Americas in the 1490s, European explorers and adventurers set out to see what they could get out of a strange new land across three thousand miles of ocean. In particular, English, French, Portuguese and Spanish all made efforts to establish colonies on the Caribbean Islands and bordering lands. The Spanish, however, pushed deeper into the American mainland, and with very small companies of soldiers, sometimes no more than a few dozen, conquered vast empires of millions of Indians.

Of particular importance to what would become the United States was the conquest of the Aztecs of Mexico by Hernando Cortez. The Aztecs had once been a poor tribe from Mexico's north, but during the 1400s they moved into Central Mexico and, in a sudden outburst of energy, managed to conquer many of the other Indian groups in the area. They went on to develop a civilized nation as large and populous as many European countries. Their capital city, Tenochtitlán (pronounced

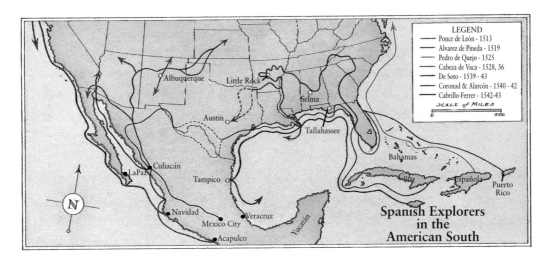

LEGEND
— Ponce de León - 1513
— Alvarez de Pineda - 1519
— Pedro de Quejo - 1525
— Cabeza de Vaca - 1528, 36
— De Soto - 1539 - 43
— Coronad & Alarcón - 1540 - 42
— Cabrillo-Ferrer - 1542-43

SCALE of MILES
0   500

Spanish Explorers
in the
American South

In the 1400s the Aztecs created a rich and prosperous society in Central Mexico. Its architecture, waterways and agricultural methods were quite advanced. Here are the ruins of the imposing temple at Malinalco.

teh-NOCK-tea-t'lan), was rich in gold and silver objects and their emperor lived in a great palace with thousands of servants attending him. Inevitably, this great wealth attracted the Spanish, and in 1521 Cortez, with a small force, conquered the Aztec kingdom and turned it into a Spanish colony. Many of the Indians were forced into slavery to work the gold and silver mines (actually the Aztecs had used prisoners of war to work the mines and the Spanish simply carried on the practice). The Aztecs, who had ruled by conquest, now saw the tables turned. The great Aztec society deteriorated: For the next three hundred years the Spanish would rule Mexico, which they called New Spain.

(above) Aztec religion was complex and often cruel. In the festival for the god Xipe Topec, prisoners of war were slain and skinned. The skins were worn by priests in ceremonies. This statue shows a priest in such a skin. The skinned hand is visible by the priest's right elbow.

(top right) Human sacrifice was an important ritual in Aztec worship. Here a victim's heart is being torn out in a sacrifice to the sun.

(below) Music was often used to accompany Aztec religious ceremonies. This small drum has H-shaped slats cut into the top, which were struck to produce different tones.

The Spanish brought to the Americas two agents of profound change. One of them was European diseases. As was true everywhere in the New World, the Indians had developed little or no natural immunity to European diseases. We are not really sure exactly why this happened. Partly it had to do with the fact that the Indians had been isolated from the Europeans for twenty thousand years or more. Partly it was because the crowded conditions of European cities made fertile breeding grounds for illnesses like smallpox and measles; Europeans often caught these diseases and over generations a certain immunity to them built up. Indians, lacking immunity to them, almost always died from the diseases—probably smallpox, measles, and bubonic plague. Right from the time of Columbus such diseases swept like wildfire through Indian towns and villages—some larger and denser than any European city—often killing 90 percent of the population in some villages and extending across thousands of square miles. (For the story of Indians' encounter with Europeans in eastern North America, readers may consult the first volume in this series, *The Clash of Cultures*). European diseases were a major factor in opening the way for the European intruders: It has been estimated that a third of the eight million Indians in Mexico died of disease within a decade after contact with the Spanish.

The second import brought to the New World by the Spanish was the horse. Actually, horses had existed in the Americas thousands of years earlier. The Indians had not tamed them, but instead had hunted them for food, and in time the horses died out. The horse proved to be a mighty weapon against the Indians, for a troop of mounted soldiers was a good match for a far larger army of foot soldiers. Horses were important to the Spanish conquest of Mexico, and the Indians quickly saw their value. They began to acquire horses by theft, battle, and trade. Eventually horses that went wild began to live in herds on the Great Plains east of the Rocky Mountains. The Plains Indians caught them and trained them, and by the 1600s the whole culture of the Plains Indians, from New Mexico up into Canada, had changed drastically. On horseback they found it easy to slaughter buffalo roaming the plains in vast herds almost at will, and there came to them a golden age of great prosperity. It is these mounted Indians following the buffalo, with their easily transportable teepees, whom Americans mainly think of when hearing the term Indian.

But while the Plains Indians did at times ride into the Southwest, the area was dominated by another people with a quite different lifestyle, who we now call Pueblo Indians, after their apartment-like dwellings made of adobe and stone plastered to cliffsides. These people had been living in what is today the southwest of the United Sates for at least eleven thousand years. They were an agricultural people whose diet was based on corn supplemented with some animal protein. They made beautiful jewelry of shell, bone, and precious minerals like jet and turquoise. They were basket makers, and also produced fine painted pottery.

FERDINANDO CORTES
CAVATO DA VN ORIGINALE FATTO INAZI
CHEI SI PORTASSI ALLA CONQVISTA DEL MESSICO

In an amazing feat of war, Hernando Cortez, with a handful of men, conquered the powerful Aztec Empire.

The drama of Cortez's famous victory over the Aztecs, and tragic fate of the defeated Indians, remains an important story in Mexican history. The modern painter Diego Rivera made this symbolic painting of Cortez's arrival at Vera Cruz.

Their famous dwellings were made up of clusters of rooms, sometimes as many as a thousand of them, stacked up in terraces. Entrance was from the top via a ladder. To Americans the best known of the Pueblo tribes were the Zuñis and the Hopis, a more isolated people farther north.

The Pueblo lands were not immediately discovered by the Spanish, who were concentrating their efforts on the rich gold and silver areas of central Mexico. Indeed the Pueblo area, what is now Arizona and New Mexico, was seen as a distant borderland about which little was known. However, there was rumored to be there the Seven Cities of Cíbolo, supposedly filled with precious metals and jewels. Probably the Pueblo Indian villages were the basis for this myth. In 1538 a Spanish explorer, Fray Marcos de Niza, marched north, where he found thousands of Indians living in pueblos. When the news got back to Mexico some people jumped to the conclusion that these were the legendary Seven Cities of Cíbolo. An expedition under Francisco Vásquez de Coronado went north to conquer them.

However, conquest proved more difficult in the border areas than it had been farther south. Indians fought back and several bloody battles took place. In the end the Spanish won, partly through force of arms and partly, as ever, through the diseases they carried, which killed many Indians.

The Spanish had not come solely for gold and silver. Many Christian groups believed that they had a duty to God to bring "heathens" into the Christian Church, to save their souls. Such groups saw the Indians as a huge number of souls waiting to be Christianized. Indeed, it went further than that: Many of the European settlers in the New World were sure that the Indians would quickly recognize the advantages of both European material goods and culture, like guns, metal tools, writing, and their religion. Soon the Indians would adopt European ways and become, in effect, European. Thus the Indian problem would be solved peaceably. In truth, the Indians for the most part had no wish to be Europeanized, but wanted rather to hang onto their ancient cultures, as do most people everywhere.

But the Spanish did not understand this, and beginning around 1580, when the Indians were by no means under Spanish control, Franciscan missionaries came into the area—now largely Arizona and New

Mexico—to convert them. They were only partly successful. Then, in 1598, the Spanish government sent Juan de Oñate to take command. He won a number of battles against the Pueblos, founded Santa Fe in present-day New Mexico, and enforced his rule on the Indians. He supported the Franciscans in their efforts to convert the Indians to Christianity.

The Pueblos were not the only Indians there. The more warlike Plains Indians, especially the Apaches and Navajos, came south frequently to plunder, or to trade meat and buffalo hides for corn. But the Pueblos dominated the area.

One critically important fact, for reasons we shall eventually see, is that Oñate, and the Spanish in general, were not primarily interested in settling the areas they had conquered. Their main objective was to take away by trade or conquest what valuables they could—gold, silver, jewels, hides, and whatever else they found. In contrast, the English who were taking over other parts of North America—though no more considerate of the Indians and their culture—were mainly settlers who hoped to earn their livings by cultivating the land and seas, and shipping back to Europe produce they harvested, like tobacco, timber, and fish.

Unfortunately for the Spanish, these borderlands conquered by Oñate, which the Spanish were calling New Mexico, did not contain many precious metals or jewels. Spanish adventurers were not attracted to the land. The Spanish government quickly concluded that New Mexico would never be profitable to them. Still, they were worried that other Europeans, especially the English and the French, would push into the area, and they decided they had to keep control of New Mexico as a buffer region to protect the much richer lands of central Mexico and farther south. They decided to use the Franciscan missionaries to settle New Mexico and convert and exploit the Indians. In the end, then, it was this religious order, not the soldiers, who took control of that part of the region that became the United States, now largely the states of Arizona and New Mexico.

But Spanish claims to the area stretched much farther than this, ranging from the Mississippi on the east, and to the west up the Pacific coast for several hundred miles. However, it was one thing to claim the land, another to possess it. Although a few Spanish explorers, like Hernando do Soto and Luis de Moscoso, came into present-day Texas and made contact with the Indians in the 1500s, the first missionary settlement was not established until 1690, over a hundred and fifty years after the earliest explorations. By 1700 there were a few Spanish missions in Texas, and over the next century missions, trading posts, and small settlements appeared here and there in eastern Texas. But the Spanish presence in Texas was never large. As one historian puts it, "Franciscans in Texas

Indians of the Great Plains acquired horses from the Spanish, and quickly became masterful horsemen. By the 1600s the Plains Indians had built a culture around horses, which they rode in battle and used to hunt the buffalo that supplied many of their needs.

suffered from many of the same impediments that missionaries had encountered in other times and places—epidemics, unruly soldiers, quarrels between representatives of the church and the state, and Indians' devotion to their own religions. . . ." But in Texas there was another element: the French in their Louisiana colony to the east. The French also wanted to trade with Indians for beaver skins and buffalo hides. They offered the Indians an alternative to the Spanish traders in Texas, and thus the Spanish were never able to dominate the Indians in Texas as they had done in the New Mexico region.

The Spanish missions were usually quite elaborate, and were modeled on monasteries back in Spain, with a number of rooms around a courtyard. They had their own vegetable gardens, herds of cattle and sheep, and needed perhaps twenty Indian servants to keep them going. Unfortunately, the Indians were expected to work for nothing. They were required to collect piñon nuts, salt and corn, wash and tan hides, weave cloth, and help to transport these products south to Mexico. In addition, Pueblo households were taxed one hide and one-and-a-half bushels of corn each per year, for support of both the missions and the governor's establishment. Other Pueblo Indians were required to work at the missions, taking care of the herds of cattle and sheep, working in the fields, serving as cooks, bell ringers, and the like.

To some extent the Indians benefited from a power struggle between the Franciscan missionaries and the governors. For example, in a few instances governors ruled that the Franciscans had to pay wages to the Indians who worked for them. But generally speaking, the Spanish bore down hard on the Indians, intent upon making them contribute as much as possible to the support of the missionaries and governors who were there to exploit them.

Because the Indians had to spend a great deal of their time working on the missions, they were forced to neglect their own homes and fields, and a great many of the Pueblos fell into poverty. Making matters worse, the Franciscans, determined to make good Christians of the Indians, tried to stamp out Indian religions. They even went into the kivas, or sacred rooms, and destroyed religious objects, like kachina masks.

The Indians by no means accepted Spanish oppression placidly. Frequently they would revolt. In particular, the Navajos and Apaches of the Plains were able to fight off Spanish domination. But this very independence of the Plains Indians worked in favor of the Spanish. Despite the fact that the Plains Indians traded regularly with the Pueblos, sometimes for Spanish tools like knives and horses, they also made raids on both the Pueblos and the Spanish settlements, usually for horses and corn. The Pueblo Indians saw the Plains Indians as enemies, even though they traded with them, and would help the Spanish to fight them. It was an old pattern: Ancient Indian rivalries frequently prevented Indian tribes from joining against the European intruders.

Needless to say, all of these Indian groups resented Spanish domination. To be sure, under pressure some of them did convert to Christianity—some may even have welcomed the new religion. And of course, like Indians everywhere, they took up Spanish customs and implements that seemed useful, like metal hoes and knives, the horse, guns, and such. But most did not convert; and many of those who did took the Christian God as an addition to their tribal worship.

From time to time the Pueblo Indians would attack and kill a few missionaries, in response to which the Spanish would execute the people they thought responsible. Occasionally the Indians would rise in open rebellion—at Zuñi in 1632, at Taos in 1639–40, at Jemez in 1644. The Hopis, isolated on a mesa at the northern edge of New Mexico, managed to hang onto their independence, agreeing to accept Christianity and Spanish authority when Spanish military showed up, and then forgetting it all when the troops left.

Then in the 1660s and 1670s problems built up. For one thing, low rainfall and high temperatures hurt crops, and there was much starvation. For another, the impoverished Pueblos had little to trade with the Plains Indians, who increasingly began to raid for what they had previously gained in trade. It seemed to the Pueblo Indians that the prayers of the Franciscans for better weather and protection from the Plains Indians were not working. They began to return to their ancient religion in hopes of better results. The Spanish reaction was to increase persecution of the Indians in order to hold them to Christianity.

In 1680 a few Pueblo Indian leaders began to meet quietly. Their plan was to make a concerted attack on the Spanish, and throw them out of New Mexico altogether. The key figure was an Indian religious leader from the Pueblo of San Juan, named Popé. Hiding in a kiva at Taos, he organized the rebellion. From here he got most of the Pueblos of New Mexico to join with him, although a few remained loyal to the Spanish. This itself was a formidable task, for the Pueblos were spread out over several hundred miles, and did not all speak the same language. Popé sent out messengers with "calendars" of knotted ropes. Each day one knot was untied, with the last one to be untied on August 11. However, the Spanish were tipped off a couple of days ahead of time, and the revolt began a day early.

Even so, the Spanish were caught off guard. The Indians swept through the Spanish villages. Individual farms and settlements fell easily. A great many of the Spanish settlers fled in a rush. At the same time the Indians laid siege to the Spanish capital at Santa Fe. They now had guns and swords they had taken from the Spanish in the first battles in the rebellion. They had two thousand warriors against one thousand Spanish in the town, among them only about a hundred soldiers. The Indians cut off the water supply, and in the end the Spanish were forced to flee. The Indians let them go down the Rio Grande to what is today Ciudad Juárez, across the river from El Paso, Texas. And within a few weeks the Spanish were gone from New Mexico north of Juárez.

The victors now turned against most things Spanish. They killed missionaries, destroyed holy objects, desecrated churches. They agreed not to speak Spanish, and they washed themselves in the rivers in order to cleanse themselves of Christianity. They did keep on with some things Spanish, like raising livestock and weaving woolen cloth. But in the main, they were determined to return to the old ways. The Pueblo rebellion was one of the few times when the Indians were able to actually drive back the onslaught of Europeans flowing into the New World.

CHAPTER II

The Creation of the Southwest Hispanic Culture

Unfortunately for the Indians, the rebellion did not stick. In 1691 a daring Spaniard named Diego de Vargas arrived at El Paso del Norte (Juárez) with a claim to lands in New Mexico now held by the Indians. Vargas was able to enlist on his side some of the Pueblo Indians who had stayed loyal to the Spanish during the rebellion, many of whom were now in El Paso. Over the next few years Vargas fought the Indians in one battle after another. The Indians were dogged and determined, and until 1694 clung to their independence. That year Vargas, with his Indian allies, attacked the capital, Sante Fe. Before the attack they prayed to a wooden New Mexican image of the Virgin Mary, known as *Nuestra Señora de la Conquista* (Our Lady of the Conquest). This time they beat the Indians, and executed seventy who had refused to surrender. Even today, "La Conquistadora" is venerated in Santa Fe.

Vargas' conquest over the Indians was not yet complete. He had to fight on for another six months, but in the end he recovered most of the old Spanish holdings in New Mexico, with only the Hopis remaining independent. One effect of war and upheaval was a substantial decrease in the population of the Pueblos, some of which were simply abandoned.

But it had not been all loss for the Indians. The Spanish now under-stood that if they ground down too hard on the Indians they would risk another rebellion, at the cost of many lives. There now began a period of accommodation, with the Spanish and Indians trying to live side by side in peace. Among other things, they needed to cooperate in order to fend off raids by the Apaches, Utes, Comanches, and Navajos of the Plains. The Spanish still tried to push the Indians into Christianity, but they tol-erated the Indians' worshiping in their old way, and while they did some-times try to force the Indians to work for them, they attempted to deal more fairly with them. The Indians, in turn, accepted the uneasy truce that prevailed: It was better than what they had before the 1680 rebellion.

The road was now open for the creation of an Hispanic culture in what would become the southwestern United States. Such a culture already existed farther south, in Mexico proper. It had come about as a natural result of colonization. European settlers everywhere in the Americas did not usually set out to build brand-new societies, but tried to re-create in the New World the societies they had left behind. For example, the English in Massachusetts and Virginia built houses like the ones in England, established English courts and English churches, used English farming methods, etc.

The Spanish did the same in their colonies. Laws, rules about land and other property, and systems of government were the same as at home. So were fashions in dress, home furnishings, festivals, and other forms of entertainment. One army officer, going off with Juan de Oñate to conquer New Mexico, took with him several pairs of cordovan leather boots, and six fancy suits, one of them of "blue velvet . . . trimmed with wide gold passementerie, consisting of doublet, breeches, and green silk stockings with blue garters with . . . gold lace." This was dress for a sol-dier going to war on the frontier.

The Indians were drawn into the Spanish culture. For one thing, Indians forced to work on the Franciscan missions inevitably learned to

The missions were critical in establishing the Hispanic culture in the Southwest. They were often quite elaborate establishments with many buildings, farms, and workshops. These are the remains of a mission church built in 1617, near what is today the town of Jemez Springs, New Mexico. The church was large and substantial.

speak some Spanish, adopted Spanish food and cooking, the Christian religion, the use of Spanish tools, and Spanish clothing. Other Indians, mostly women and children, came into Spanish homes as slaves, and they, too, learned Spanish ways. Still other Indians, during the colonial fighting, sided with the Spanish. After the Pueblo revolution of 1680 many of them moved to El Paso and merged into the Spanish culture. Many took Spanish names.

Not all Indians, as we have seen, rejoiced in Spanish ways; many made a point of rejecting the Spanish culture in favor of the ancient Indian life. But even those Indians had to learn a little Spanish in order to trade, and although they kept to their traditional farming methods, they found Spanish tools, like metal hoes, knives, axes, etc. useful.

The mixing was not just cultural; it was biological as well. It was always the case everywhere in the European colonization of the Americas

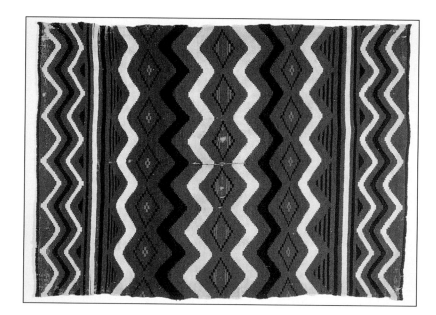

Even though the Spanish dominated the area, and made profound changes to the Indian culture, much of that culture remained. The Navajo sarape poncho here, woven in the mid-1800s, long after the Spanish conquest of the area, shows ancient patterns from the Indian past.

that the first wave consisted mainly, if not entirely, of men—soldiers, sailors, explorers, adventurers hoping to get rich. These men might be gone from home for years. They took Indian girlfriends, and frequently married Indian women. In time a population of people of mixed blood developed.

This process of racial mixing certainly took place in Mexico. Very quickly there came into being a substantial population of mixed Indian and Spanish blood. In time a small number of black slaves were added to the mix. These racially mixed people often intermarried, and in the end, the basic population of Mexico (or New Spain as the Spanish called it) came to be these *mestizos*, as they came to be called. Mixed in among them were many purebred Indians, who to one extent or another had adopted Spanish ways. Also part of the mix were a minority of pure Spanish descent, generally called *españoles*.

Taken together, the biological and cultural mixing that now existed in Mexico (and elsewhere in Spanish America) created an Hispanic culture that was similar to the culture of Spain, but significantly modified by the cultures of the Indians and the blacks who were part of it. For example, the traditional Indian diet based on corn and beans became a staple of the Hispanic culture. Buildings were often made of adobe, the local material well adapted to a dry climate. Silver, flowing from the Mexican mines, was widely used in Indian decoration. Moccasins were widely used. It was a two-way street, with influences flowing both ways.

This Hispanic society, as is usually the case, was divided. At the top of the pile were the minority of pure Spanish descent, who usually had the most important jobs in government, the army, and the church. In fact, the colony was largely ruled by Spaniards sent over specifically to fill various government offices.

Below these españoles were the mestizos, and at the bottom were the Africans and pureblood Indians, many of them slaves. This social arrangement was not just convention, but was written into law. For example, the españoles could not be publicly flogged for crimes, but everybody else could. The españoles generally lived around the central plazas of cities, where much of the public life was conducted; the rest lived farther out.

As is also often the case in human society, those lower down the scale tried to move themselves up. This was especially possible on the frontiers, where a rough democracy usually existed. Many mestizos started claiming that they were españoles, and many Indians and others with some black heritage claimed to be mestizos. Social distinctions began to break down. One Antonio Salazar of Zacatecas, a master mason, is listed in various documents as Indian, mestizo, and españole. A lieutenant governor of Texas, Antonio Gil Ybarbo, was known to be a mulatto—that is, part black—but was listed officially as an españole.

For students of American history, the key point is that this Hispanic culture, which developed in Mexico in the 1600s and spread into New Mexico and Texas in the 1700s, was solidly in place for at least a century before any of the Southwest was taken over by the United States. It must be admitted that this Hispanic population in the Southwest was very small. As late as 1765 there were fewer than ten thousand Hispanics in New Mexico, a third of them in the El Paso district. There were also about ten thousand Hispanic Indians mixed in. There were fewer Hispanics than this in Texas, very few at all in Southern California, and hardly any farther north along the California coast. Nonetheless, the Hispanics had taken over from the Indians, established their own way of life, and there has continued to be an Hispanic element in the culture of the American Southwest into the present.

We must keep it in mind that so far as the Spanish back in Spain were concerned, Mexico, Texas, and the New Mexico area were all of a piece—one huge colony, almost two thousand miles from tip to toe. The colonial government was centered in Mexico City, where Spanish governors and other officials dwelt in considerable splendor. The Catholic Church was almost equal in power to the government officials, and the church, too, had its splendid buildings.

But a great many people, especially the mestizos, who were by far the majority, were poor, some of them desperately so. Part of the problem was the usual one with European colonies: So far as kings, queens, rich merchants in Europe were concerned, the colonies were there to enrich the homelands. The rulers back home were not much concerned about the problems of people laboring to enrich themselves five thousand miles away. Neither were the officials they sent out to govern the colonies interested in building a sound society. They came to make their fortunes, and hoped to go home as soon as they had done so. They were often corrupt, taking huge bribes from merchants and traders who wanted special rights to this or that sort of trade. In sum, in Mexico, as in many New World colonies, the rulers were rich and imperious, the ordinary people downtrodden. It was a situation ripe for rebellion.

In 1775 the revolution of British colonies along the Atlantic seaboard began, and in six years the Americans had beaten the British army, considered the mightiest in the world. Everywhere in the American colonies people took heart. A few years later, in 1789, the French people revolted against their oppressive government. They, too, won. However, out of the confusion of the French Revolution there arose a dictator, Napoléon Bonaparte, a man of enormous ambition, who set out to rule all of Europe, if not the world. Napoleon soon conquered Spain.

In the Spanish colonies it was clear to people that they could take advantage of the turmoil in Europe: The Spanish and the French, preoccupied with their own wars, were not in a position to put down rebellions thousands of miles away. Revolutionary movements began in several colonies, notably the French colony of Haiti. And in 1810, an independence movement began in Mexico. For awhile the rebels were triumphant, but eventually the government forces won, and the independence spirit flickered low. It did not die out, however. Spain itself was swept by revolutionary fervor, with governments rising and falling. There was nothing it could do to hold Mexico, and in 1821 an independent Mexican Empire was established.

But this did not end the turmoil in Mexico, for now that the country was an independent nation, many ambitious men with their own armies began to struggle for power. These people, too, were mainly concerned about their own interests, rather than the good of the mass of the people, or the country as a whole. Governments rose and fell. Ultimately Antonio López de Santa Anna, a successful general, emerged as a dominant figure, but even he went in and out of power.

Meanwhile, movements were taking place in both the United States and the Texas portion of the Mexican Empire that would have profound effects on American history and the shape of our country today. For one thing, the population of the United States east of the Mississippi was exploding. This was due in part to immigrants pouring in, but mainly because of natural fertility—American families were simply having a lot

West front of Church.

(above) A general view of the Alamo Mission, probably engraved not long after the fight there. (below) An artist's imaginative drawing of the death of Davy Crockett at the Alamo, showing the Mexican soldiers swarming into the mission.

of children, and because there was plenty of food and a low rate of disease, the infant death rate was low, compared with that of other countries. All these new people needed farmland, which was in short supply in the older states along the Atlantic Coast.

Second, in 1803 President Thomas Jefferson arranged for the purchase of the huge Louisiana Territory, once Spanish, but at the moment controlled by the French dictator, Napoleon Bonaparte. (For the story of the Louisiana Purchase, see the volume in this series called *The Jeffersonian Republicans*.) This enormous piece of land covered everything from Texas up to Canada between the Mississippi and the Rocky Mountains. With the Louisiana Purchase the United States, not France, lay along the northern border of the Mexican Empire. Through the years after the Louisiana Purchase, Americans, especially in bordering Louisiana, kept eyeing the vast Texas land, with its tiny Hispanic population and roving Indian bands. Several adventurers went into Texas to see what they could take.

The Spanish were not eager to fill their lands with foreigners, but on the other hand, they realized that they had to colonize the Texas area if they wished to hang onto it. So in 1820 they gave Moses Austin of Connecticut permission to settle three hundred families in the region between the Brazos and Colorado Rivers in Texas. Austin died before he could take anybody out to Texas, but in 1821 his son Stephen Austin got the Spanish contract confirmed by the now independent Mexican government. Thus the American settlement of Texas, a part of Mexico, began.

The land was suitable for growing cotton, a crop on which planters in the southern United States were making money and in some cases growing rich. It was also a natural country for sheep and cattle. Americans flooded in. At first the Mexican government welcomed the immigrants and granted them land. But there were only four thousand Hispanics in Texas, almost all of them in the southwestern part of the

province. Soon the Americans in their enclave to the north outnumbered the Hispanics. Moreover, the Americans were building a separate society. They did not bother to learn Spanish but spoke English. They attempted to build their own school system and arranged for their own defense against the Indians. Within ten years they outnumbered the Hispanics in Texas ten to one.

The Mexican government tried to assert control over the incoming Americans; the Americans resisted. They had formed a compact society and did not want to be ruled from Mexico City, a thousand miles away. There was tension, sporadic fighting, and finally, in 1835, open rebellion. On March 2, 1836, the Texans declared their independence.

Mexico was determined to hang onto the province, and sent a large army north to subdue the rebellious Americans. The army approached San Antonio, one of the larger towns of Texas. It was lightly defended. The Texas volunteers holed up in a former mission, which had been fortified, called the Alamo. The handful of defenders refused to surrender, and vowed to fight to the death. That they did, fighting hand to hand with knives, swords, and pistols. Among the dead were such legendary Americans as Davy Crockett, Jim Bowie, and William B. Travis. The brave, indeed foolhardy, defense of the Alamo aroused the ire of the American Texans. After a few setbacks, the Americans, under Sam Houston, took on the Mexican army at San Jacinto. They went into battle crying, "Remember the Alamo," now one of the most famous of all American war cries, and defeated the Mexicans. Texas was now free and independent, a nation of its own—but run by former citizens of the United States. Hispanic control of the American Southwest, after three hundred years, was coming to an end.

CHAPTER III

Manifest Destiny

W e must now step back a pace and look at the situation that existed in North America at the moment that Texas got its independence from Mexico. Officially, the territory of the United States ran westward to a rather vague line along the Red River bordering Texas, and up the Rocky Mountains to the Canada border. Everything west of this line either belonged to other nations, or was at least claimed by them. Mexico extended north through the New Mexico area. That country also claimed, and controlled, substantial portions of what is now California, up to about San Francisco. The land farther north—today Northern California, Oregon, and Washington as well as parts of states like Idaho and Colorado—was claimed by the Russians, who held Alaska and could honestly say that they were the closest European nation to the area; and by England, whose fur trappers and traders had been dealing with the Indians in the Northwest from Canadian bases for decades. Clearly, a number of other nations had better claims of one kind or another to the western part of the continent than the United States had.

But that was not how Americans saw it. For one thing, it had been clear from the outset that the Americans in Texas did not really want an independent nation; they really wanted to join the United States, and in 1836 the Texas legislature voted to ask the U. S. government to take it in as a new state. This did not happen, for reasons we shall look at later; but most Americans and Texans took it for granted that it soon would happen.

More important, the American population was growing at a fantastic rate—doubling every twenty-five years. (In comparison, it took over sixty years for the population to double after 1930.) On this basis people were calculating that the population would reach 300 million in a hundred years (it has not reached that figure yet), and that the country would need all that empty land out west to supply farms for those people.

And indeed Americans were moving west, as they always had, pushing out into the lands across the Mississippi to scratch out farms, regardless of the claims of other nations, or the rights of Indians who lived there. Pioneers were making the long, dangerous trek into the fertile

Americans began to pour westward to the Pacific Coast beginning in the 1830s, when the claims of the United States to the area were not very good. This drawing, made in 1830, shows covered wagons moving in a mob across the prairie, headed for Oregon.

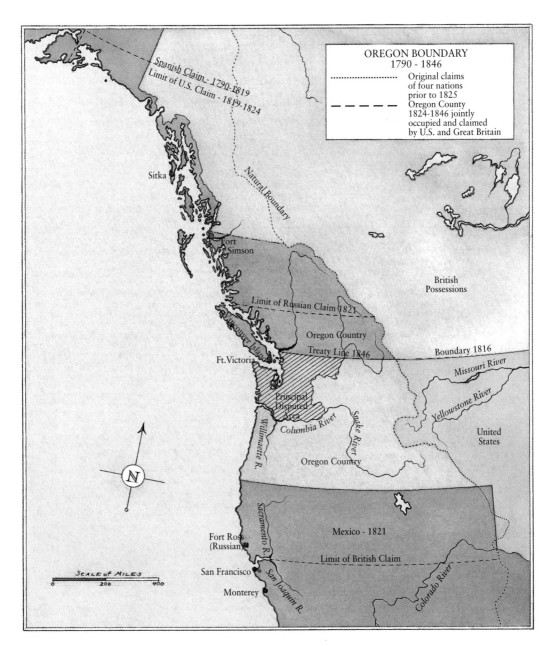

Oregon Territory (now the Northwest). They were traveling out of Louisiana and the South generally into Texas. They were coming from everywhere into the Great Plains, what is today the tier of states from the Dakotas down to Oklahoma.

Americans much admired these pioneers. There was something very attractive about the pioneering spirit, which encouraged people to venture into new and dangerous lands to build something for themselves. Indeed, it almost seemed that the pioneering spirit typified America: It was part of what the nation was all about. Thus, even when the pioneers were venturing into lands they had little or no right to, Americans applauded them.

It was very much in this spirit that in 1845 a newspaper editorialist wrote that it was "our manifest destiny to overspread the continent allotted by Providence for the free development of our yearly multiplying millions." God Himself, according to this editorial writer, had ordained that the whole continent should become American. The phrase *manifest destiny* caught on. It meant that it was America's "obvious fate" to take over all the land to the Pacific. By this way of thinking, as it was our *destiny*, we must have a *right* to it. Needless to say, this was not quite so obvious to the Spanish, English, and Russians, nor to the Indians who had once thought it was their manifest destiny to live on that land.

Americans romanticized the pioneers, and especially the hunters and trappers who proceeded them into the mountains. Here is one of these rough, tough mountain men, Kan Foster, looking indomitable despite his tattered clothing.

To some extent the phrase "manifest destiny" was an excuse for a simple land grab. The rich, fertile lands of the west coast, the fine harbors there, the furs and hides, the potential for whaling and fishing in general, the possibilities of valuable minerals in the mountains of the Southwest were great attractions to merchants, shippers, and investors. Why should the English and the Spanish exploit these commercial possibilities? Add to this the enormous demand for southern cotton created by the booming textile industry. There were fortunes to be made by cotton growers using slave labor, if they could find good land in a hot climate. Eastern Texas contained millions of acres of such land. Finally, given the population explosion, the United States would be well advised to get hold of any open land it could, just in case.

Whaling was highly dangerous work, but extremely profitable. Gaining ports for ships was one of the lures the Pacific Coast had for Americans.

But there was more to manifest destiny than wealth and practicalities. Americans have always been known for their commonsensical, hard-headed, practical ways. But there has been another side to America that is often overlooked. We have also been a nation of dreamers, of people eager to embark on glorious adventures, build new and better ways, not for profit, but just to do something great. The Puritans who made the dangerous crossing from England to an even more dangerous land did so not for money, but in order to build a City on the Hill, as they put it, which would be an example to the world. The men who wrote the Constitution and formed the new nation were also not doing it for profit, but with the dream in mind of creating the best and most free nation the world had ever seen.

This same feeling of being part of a great and glorious adventure was mixed into the idea of manifest destiny. Americans felt that they had created a great democratic nation, profoundly different from others around the world. They had not merely a right but a *duty* to spread this nation and its ideals far and wide. The idea of America's manifest destiny to take over the whole continent, then, expressed both sides of the American spirit—the practical, hardheaded side that said we had better get hold of this immensely valuable western land before somebody else does, and the spiritual side that said that we had a duty to give the benefit of American ideals to the world.

Not all Americans liked the idea of manifest destiny. There were a good many who felt that the United States had no right to grab land that other nations, especially Mexico, had perfectly good claims to. Especially, they believed that the Indians were once again going to be pushed off land that was theirs. But that was a minority view: The majority of Americans believed in manifest destiny.

Americans, then, were determined to push west to the Pacific. But how, as a practical matter, to do it? The Russians were not really much of a threat, although they were trying to trade along the California coast

American rights to the Pacific coastlands west of the Rocky Mountains were dubious at best, but the nation had acquired much of the land across the Mississippi east of the Rockies through the Louisiana Purchase. Both private speculators and government agencies set up posts on the Plains to aid the overlanders. Here a wagoneer loads up with supplies at one such post, while Indians watch in the foreground.

and had established stockaded forts there. The English were more of a problem, because they had set up trading posts in the northwest, and were on good terms with the local Indians.

The major roadblock to manifest destiny was Mexico. The country had an old and rich culture. The University of Mexico had been founded eighty-five years before there were any colleges in North America. The capital, Mexico City, had fine buildings, churches, libraries, etc.

But there were weaknesses in the society. For one, the nation had been a colony for three hundred years, run mainly by officials sent over from Spain. The locals, thus, had not had much experience in running a government. With independence, the ethnic españoles and the *criollos* (people of Spanish parents, but born in America) took over. With little experience or tradition of home rule, they allowed things to fall into near chaos. Strongmen jostled for power, and governments came and went: Between 1833 and 1855 the presidency changed hands thirty-six times. The ruthless, charismatic, wily Santa Anna managed to dominate the government at frequent intervals, but he fell from power from time to time.

The contending strongmen had no more interest in the unhappy condition of the mestizos than had the Spanish rulers before them. So far as the powerful people were concerned, the mestizos were to be kept down. As a consequence, the bulk of the Mexican population did not have much love for their rulers.

If Mexico had been successful in colonizing its borderlands of Texas,

Perhaps the most famous of these posts was Fort Laramie, on the Platte River, which over the years gave support and a resting place to tens of thousands of pioneers.

New Mexico, and California, the story might have had a different end-ing. But in the early 1800s people in central Mexico saw the distant bor-derlands as wild and uncivilized country, scantily settled by rough pio-neers and dangerous Indians. A civilized person would be foolish to visit the area, much less settle there. So they did not. As late as the 1830s there were only about four thousand Hispanics in Texas, though there were forty-four thousand in New Mexico, most in the upper Rio Grande Valley, north of Albuquerque. In California there were only a handful of Hispanics in the 1820s. Control was exerted through four *presidios*, or forts, spaced along the hundreds of miles of coast between San Diego and San Francisco. The presidios protected twenty-one Franciscan missions. At times there were only *thirty-six* missionaries running these missions, but incredibly, with the help of the soldiers from the presidios, they con-trolled some *twenty thousand* Indians who worked virtually as slaves on the vast cattle, sheep, pig, and horse ranches that were making the mis-sions rich. The Indians fared no better when civil officers replaced the priests and friars as heads of the California missions in the 1830s.

Americans looked on their neighbor to the south with contempt. They saw a Mexican nation in turmoil, unable to govern itself, peopled by a downtrodden peasantry. The contrast with the United States, where a sound government was answerable to a largely literate, free population was stark. And herein lay the difference. Americans were free to pick up and move on, to settle almost anywhere they wanted if they could make a go of it. For ordinary Mexicans moving was difficult. Their lives were largely controlled by the authorities over them—the great landowners, the generals, the church, and government officials. Moreover, it was very difficult for a common Mexican to stake a claim to land anywhere. Most of the land was given out by the government to wealthy españoles who were supposed to settle farmers on it. But the few who tried to develop their lands on the borders used them to create vast ranches for cattle, horses, sheep, and hogs. There were great fortunes to be made by a

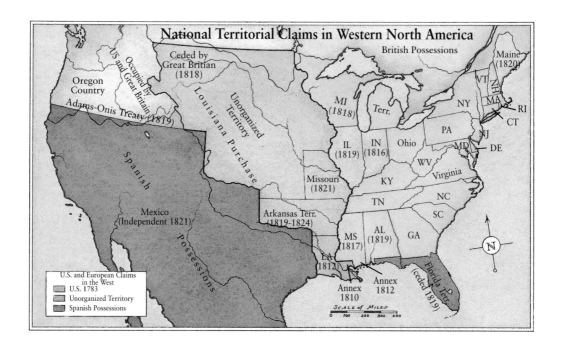

favored few in this system, but the land remained unpeopled: As we have seen, the Mexican government had to bring in Americans to settle Texas.

In general, Mexico, both under the Spanish and as an independent nation, had seen these borderlands of Texas, New Mexico, and California mainly as buffers to keep out Russians from the north, Americans from the east and Indians from both directions. There were just not enough people in Mexico to pursue the Spanish objectives of Christianizing the Indians, spreading Spanish culture, and exploiting natural resources. In addition, the borderlands were a thousand miles from Mexico City, at a time when it took weeks to travel that far. Mexicans had far more important things than the development and control of Texas to concern themselves with at home, particularly in the decades after independence, when contentious strongmen were plunging the nation into chaos. The Mexicans, then, had left themselves in a bad situation in their borderlands; and now they were faced with an expansion-minded United States claiming it had a manifest destiny to push on to the Pacific Ocean.

CHAPTER IV

The War with Mexico

Few events in American history have proven so controversial as the Mexican War. Even as it was being fought a great many Americans opposed it, saying it was simply a war of aggression against a neighboring nation that really could not be justified. Nonetheless, the majority of Americans supported it, for good reasons and bad, and the first historians to write about it presented it as a glorious adventure ending with a grand American victory. Later historians took the opposite view: The Mexican War was an open grab for a vast amount of territory that Mexico had perfectly good rights to. Today historians take a somewhat more balanced position: While it is hard to justify the war with Mexico in moral terms, there are nonetheless some grounds on which the takeover of California and the Southwest seem reasonable—and certainly in the best interests of the United States.

The path to the war was opened when Texas won its own rebellion against Mexico. It established itself as an independent republic and elected President Andrew Jackson's old friend Sam Houston as its first president. Immediately both Texans and many Americans began demanding that Texas be admitted to the United States. There were, beyond the emotional

THE GREEDY BOY.

These cartoons show two attitudes toward the Mexican War. At left, Queen Victoria and Prince Albert of England are reprimanding a boy intent upon eating up Mexico, California, and Texas. Below, a patriotic cartoon shows the Mexican eagle full of fight before the war, and plucked of its feathers after it.

PLUCKED:

OR.

THE MEXICAN EAGLE BEFORE THE WAR!   THE MEXICAN EAGLE AFTER THE WAR!

idea of manifest destiny, some more practical reasons for admitting Texas to the Union. For one thing, England had a considerable interest in Texas. Its huge textile industry needed mountains of American cotton. Texas was cotton country, and England saw commercial advantages in making deals with an independent Texas for cotton and other goods. The United States did not want England meddling in Texas, and statehood for Texas would eliminate the threat.

But the possibility of statehood for Texas raised another contentious issue. Texas had been settled mainly by Southerners and many Texans owned slaves.

For a variety of reasons, the North and the South were rivals. They had different climates, different ways of life, different economies, and most particularly, one area had slavery, the other did not. Right from the time of the writing of the Constitution, American governments had been careful to keep the power of North and South in balance. In practical terms this meant that there had to be as many slave states as there were free ones. Because the North was more populous, it had a majority in the House of Representatives. However, if there were equal numbers of slave and free states, the South would have half the senators, which—because of special debating and voting rules—would in practice give it a veto over laws passed by the House. Needless to say, it was critically important to the South to see that for every free state that was admitted, a slave state was admitted at the same time.

In the North, however, by the time of Texas independence, the opposition to slavery was steadily growing. Many Northerners had come to feel strongly against slavery, and were opposed to seeing it spread into new territories and states. Both sides cared deeply about this issue, and it was never going to be easy to find a compromise. (For a discussion of this problem, readers may consult the volume in this series called *Slavery and the Coming of the Civil War*.)

It was obvious to everybody that the land out there in the west could be carved into a great many states—in fact, when Texas was finally admitted in 1845, the terms said that it could be cut into as many as five states. But no states were going to be admitted until the question of whether they would be free states or slave was settled. For political reasons, Presidents Andrew Jackson and Martin Van Buren were loath to start what would be a bitter debate dividing the Democratic Party and, indeed, the nation; each decided to put off statehood for Texas.

There was a second reason for delaying the annexation of Texas: It would almost certainly bring on a war with Mexico. But pressure for annexation was growing and it could not be postponed indefinitely. And in February 1845 Congress passed a resolution calling for the admission of Texas to the Union. Mexico immediately protested, and withdrew its ambassador from Washington. President James K. Polk sent troops to the Mexican border and naval ships to the Mexican coast.

Making matters worse, the Texas nation was claiming a much larger piece of land than the original Texas of 1836 had been. The old border was supposed to be the Nueces River. Now Texas was

President James K. Polk would avoid a war with Mexico if he could, but he was determined to acquire for the United States the valuable western lands held by Mexico. He was willing to fight if he had to.

claiming all the land to the Rio Grande, a huge piece of country that included chunks of New Mexico and towns like Albuquerque, Santa Fe, and Taos. This new claim by itself was twice the size of the original Texas. With the admission of Texas as a new state, the American government supported this claim to all the land south to the Rio Grande.

Nonetheless, Polk wanted to avoid war if he could, and he sent a special envoy, John Slidell, to Mexico City to see if he could negotiate a border settlement and smooth things over in general. Slidell also had secret orders from Polk to offer to buy both California and New Mexico from Mexico—five million dollars for New Mexico, and twenty-five million for California. Unfortunately for everybody, news of this effort by America to buy vast pieces of Mexican land leaked out. The newspapers raged against the whole idea, and the Mexican government broke off negotiations.

But the Mexicans then played right into American hands. A Mexican general decided at this crucial moment to use his troops to take over the government over a thousand miles away in Mexico City. Once again Mexico was in political chaos, opening a door for the United States. Despite the chaos, both the Mexican government and the Mexican people strongly favored war against an America that was determined, as they saw it, to carve up Mexico. The giant to the north had to be taught a lesson. And the Mexicans believed they could win such a war. The United States was quarreling with England over Oregon, and might have a war on its hands there. There was also reason to believe that Mexico would get support from the French.

Further, Mexicans believed, as their troops marched in triumph through Texas, Indians would join them, making up a great army that would sweep on to New Orleans. Moreover, Mexico would be fighting near to home, close to its sources of supply; the Americans would be fighting three thousand miles from their capital city. On top of everything, Mexico had a large and experienced army, hardened from years of

VOLUNTEERS !

Men of the Granite State!
Men of Old Rockingham!! the
strawberry-bed of patriotism, renowned for bravery and devotion to Country, rally at this call. Santa Anna, reeking with the generous confidence and magnanimity of your countrymen, is in arms, eager to plunge his traitor-dagger in their bosoms. To arms, then, and rush to the standard of the fearless and gallant **CUSHING**---put to the blush the dastardly meanness and rank toryism of Massachusetts. Let the half civilized Mexicans hear the crack of the unerring New Hampshire rifleman, and illustrate on the plains of San Luis Potosi, the fierce, determined, and undaunted bravery that has always characterized her sons.

Col. **THEODORE F. ROWE**, at No. 31 Daniel-street, is authorized and will enlist men this week for the Massachusetts Regiment of Volunteers. The compensation is **$10 per month---$30 in advance.** Congress will grant a handsome bounty in money and **ONE HUNDRED AND SIXTY ACRES OF LAND.**

Portsmouth, Feb. 2. 1847.

The majority of Americans, filled with the idea that America had a "manifest destiny" to reach from sea to sea, were ready to fight. This poster calling for volunteers refers to the Mexicans as "half civilized," and claims that Santa Anna was "eager to plunge his traitor-dagger" into American breasts.

internal battling, which was in any case much larger than the American army. The Americans would be depending on ill-trained militia and hastily recruited volunteers, who would have to march through deserts and cross mountains to invade Mexico. It did not seem possible for Mexico to lose a war with the United States. And so, instead of looking for a peaceful solution, the Mexicans decided to take a tough stance.

In truth, America was more split over the coming war than Mexico was: A lot of people—especially in the North—continued to be against it. Nonetheless, President Polk ordered General Zachary Taylor to lead his troops into the disputed ground between the Nueces and the Rio Grande. At what is now Brownsville, Texas, the Mexican commander told him to withdraw, but Taylor refused. There was a skirmish, and a few Americans were killed. Polk now told Congress, "We have tried every effort at reconciliation . . . but now, after reiterated menaces, Mexico has passed the boundary of the United States, has invaded our territory, and shed American blood on American soil."

This statement was sheer nonsense. Americans had marched into territory that had always been considered Mexican, to which Americans had only the flimsiest claims. But Polk's patriotic exhortation was enough to tip the balance in Congress, and war was declared. The Mexican response was to bring back the opportunistic Santa Anna and put him in charge of the army.

President Polk organized a three-pronged attack. One prong would move into New Mexico and California; another would slice into northern Mexico; and a third would come by ship to central Mexico and fight its way to the capital, Mexico City. For the Americans the war got off to a good start. Then the Mexican governor of New Mexico surrendered Santa Fe without a shot—he may have accepted a bribe. Some *Californios* (California-born Hispanics) put up a stiff but very brief resistance, but California fell, too, and suddenly the United States had possession of much of the Southwest.

The second prong, under General Zachary Taylor, with six thousand troops, moved into Mexico from the north, heading to Monterey. Against them stood seven thousand Mexicans. For three days there was heavy fighting, with a lot of casualties on both sides, but in the end the Mexicans were forced to surrender Monterey.

Taylor now marched his forces on to Buena Vista. Here he was met by Santa Anna, but inexplicably, after some sharp fighting Santa Anna pulled back, and took his troops down to Mexico City. The fighting had been, for the Americans, harder in northern Mexico than it had been in California, but they had achieved a quick victory.

But much harder fighting was to come. On March 9, 1847, General Winfield Scott landed a force of ten thousand men at Vera Cruz, on the eastern coast of Mexico, unopposed. The walled city was well defended. Scott decided not to attack it directly, but circled around behind it and settled in to shell it into submission. For two days he poured sixty-seven hundred shells into Vera Cruz, killing not only soldiers but civilians as

This rare photograph, one of the first ever made of a war scene, shows General Robert C. Wood, Zachary Taylor's son-in-law, with his staff in the Mexican town of Salito.

well, including hundreds of women and children. Finally, as supplies began to run out and bodies to pile up in the streets, Vera Cruz gave in.

Scott now began to march toward Mexico City. At Puebla he was met by a force under Santa Anna, which he quickly routed. He then fought his way up through the mountains that surrounded the Mexican plateau, and there, laid out before him as on a giant map, was Mexico City. He could expect Mexico City to be strongly defended. Fortunately for him, but not for Santa Anna, Mexican politics were in chaos once again. Some of the Mexican states refused to support the Santa Anna leadership, and would not send money or troops to the capital. Mexico City's own government insisted that the capital could not be defended, and refused to help, whereupon Santa Anna put the city under martial law and conscripted men by force.

The fighting took place mainly on the outskirts of the city. In the district of Churubusco, it took hours of hand-to-hand combat for the

A portrait of Zachary Taylor, sitting outside his tent during the Mexican War. Taylor became so celebrated for his victories in Mexico that he was elected president two years after the war.

Americans to force the Mexicans to yield. After Churubusco, Santa Anna agreed to negotiate, but he used the time spent talking to rebuild his defenses. There followed a bloody battle at Molina del Rey, which was won by the Americans. At that point Mexico City was defended by only one strong point, the Castle at Chapultepec, which among others, contained a number of young cadets in training, most of them teenagers.

Scott began by bombarding the castle with cannon fire, hoping to reduce it without having to make a direct attack, as he had at Vera Cruz. But this time the bombardment was not enough. On September 7, 1847, a direct attack began. Fighting was fierce. Finally the Americans were able to shove fifty ladders against the castle walls. Soldiers swarmed up them, and poured over the wall. Then followed vicious hand-to-hand fighting through the streets of the castle. The defenders fought valiantly. Among them were some teenagers who chose to die rather than surrender. When it was clear that the Americans had won, according to legend,

An artist's version of the American attack on the Castle of Chapultepec. We can see the steep walls from which some of the young cadets are said to have flung themselves rather than surrender.

one of the cadets wrapped himself in a Mexican flag and flung himself off the wall to his death. Today these cadets are remembered in Mexican history as the *Niños Héroes*—the heroic children.

With the American victory at Chapultepec, the Mexican War was over. It had been a short but bloody war. Had Mexico had a strong, stable government, the United States could not have won so easily, if it could have won the war at all. And indeed, against a resolute Mexican government, the United States might have thought twice about starting the war in the first place.

At the close of the war, representatives of Mexico and the United States sat down to negotiate a treaty in the village of Guadalupe Hidalgo, just outside Mexico City. The resulting pact, ratified by the U. S. Senate in 1848, is still known as the Treaty of Guadalupe Hidalgo. It gave Texas, New Mexico, and California to the United States. In return the Americans

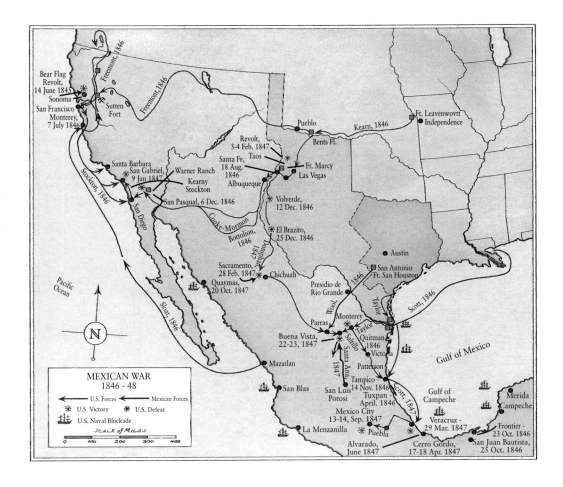

paid the Mexican government $15 million dollars, and agreed to pay off $3,250,000 in other claims American citizens had against Mexico.

The consequences of the Mexican War were tremendous. It gave the United States what it really had wanted all along, all of New Mexico and California, linking the Atlantic to the Pacific. Had this vast territory remained Mexican, and been developed by Mexicans, the history of both nations would have been much different. For one thing, the gold that was discovered in California only months after the Treaty of Guadalupe Hidalgo was signed would have streamed into Mexico, instead of the

United States. Mexico would have controlled the important port of San Francisco, through which flowed much trade to China and the East, and would have had the benefit of the great ranch lands of the Southwest. Now all of these belonged to Americans.

Nor was that the end of American acquisition of Mexican land. Santa Anna, in office again after a few years in exile, soon spent the millions he had been paid by the United States. In order to stave off his creditors, in 1853 he sold the United States the Mesilla Valley westward to and along the Gila River area along the southern borders of what are now Arizona and New Mexico. Through this so-called Gadsden Purchase the United States got the land it wanted for a railroad to California. (James Gadsden was the American minister to Mexico who carried out the negotiations.)

A second result of the Mexican War was its legacy of bad feeling. To this day many Mexicans feel bitter about the loss of a half of their country's territory to the aggressors to the north. Americans, in their turn, said that the whole episode showed simply that Mexicans were unable to govern themselves properly. Both sides ended up looking down on each other, a situation that persists today.

What, then, about the moral question? Can America's war against Mexico be justified? On the one hand, there is no question that Polk and the majority of Americans believed that the United States's manifest destiny was to take over all of the western lands from Puget Sound down to Southern California, or indeed, even more. Many Christian Americans even believed that this destiny was ordained by God. Mexican claims to some of this land, like Northern California, were in dispute; but nobody had ever doubted that the New Mexico area was Mexican. American claims there could not be justified.

Texas was another matter. The Texans had won their independence fair and square. Mexico's inability to colonize its border areas had led to the problem in the first place.

Finally, had Mexico been able to put together a stable government that could have negotiated the disputed areas with the Americans, war might have been avoided; and certainly Mexico would have lost less land than it did. In the end, while American aggressiveness was a major cause of the Mexican War, it is also true that mistakes and failures by Mexico were partly to blame, too.

Beyond the moral question, there is no getting around the fact that it was the Americans, not the Mexicans, who were settling the Southwest. In a generation the Americans had settled ten times the land there that Mexicans had over two centuries. In California it would be the same story—Americans rapidly filled a new country that the Mexicans had hardly touched. Right or wrong, it was almost inevitable that Americans, with their optimism, drive, and spirit of manifest destiny backed up by the government and fast-growing population, would push into land the Mexicans had left largely undeveloped.

And there is also no getting around the fact that wars of conquest were hardly invented by Americans. The Aztecs were a warlike people who had pushed other Indians out of Central Mexico and taken it for themselves. The Spanish in turn had slaughtered and enslaved the Aztecs. The Mexicans in their turn had thrown off Spanish rule, meanwhile keeping mestizos and Indians in peonage. The American conquest of the Southwest was just one more in a long, unhappy chain of conquest, which nobody can take much pride in.

CHAPTER V

California, Here I Come

The world was slow to discover California. It took centuries for European traders to learn of the valuable furs and other goods there, and not until two hundred and fifty years after European settlement of the East Coast of America was begun was there any real settlement of California. Even the Spanish, who under European theories of international law owned California, ignored it. By the time of the Mexican War, there were only a few thousand Hispanics in California, spread out between San Diego and San Francisco. The land lay ripe, ready to be wrested from its Indian inhabitants by anyone who had the energy and resources to do so. The story of why this was so is at the heart of the first part of California's history.

Like the rest of the New World, California was originally occupied by Indians. Because of the mild climate and the abundance of natural foods, the Indians were more thickly settled there than anywhere else in North America. The Indians were not mainly farmers, growing corn as did the Indians of the Pueblos and the East Coast. Instead they were "hunting and gathering" people, who ate seeds, acorns, roots, berries. They also fished and collected shellfish, like the crabs so abundant in the Pacific

The Indians of California were a hunting and gathering people, and thus had need of containers for the shellfish, seeds, nuts, and other items they collected. This basket is typical of their fine work. It was made by Hupa Indians of northwestern California at the end of the 1800s, but is in the style of earlier times.

The California Indians brought imagination to even the most ordinary utensils. These Karuk spoons are made of elk horn and have fanciful carved handles.

Ocean. They hunted the plentiful deer, elk, and birds, as well as seals and otters that were thick in places on the coast and offshore islands. They were masterful basket makers, and like Indians elsewhere, were skilled at making stone tools and curing hides for clothing and shelter.

California Indians were not usually joined into large confederations or nations like the Iroquois of the Northeast. Nor did they unite related bands to fight or expand as the Sioux did on the Great Plains. The

California Indians were organized instead in some sixty tribes speaking ninety languages. Although there was a lot of trading between villages up and down the coast for goods like shells and obsidian for jewelry, baskets, and bowls, each group generally stuck to its own carefully defined territory. Moreover, penned in as they were by the sea to the west and the Sierra Nevada Mountains to the east, they had little contact with the rest of the Indians of North America, who had quite different ways of life. Nonetheless, the Indians of California had rich cultures, based on strong religious beliefs, myths, legends, rituals. They played a number of different sports and games, gambled, enjoyed music. The California tribes, thus, blessed with a warm climate and plenty of natural resources, lived relatively easy and comfortable lives.

That was to change. Explorers and *conquistadores* searching for new lands that might yield some sort of riches pushed northward from Mexico. In 1533 Spanish adventurers discovered *Baja*, or Lower, California. Through the 1500s a number of ships made landings on the California coast, most of them Spanish and English. These explorers reported on the mild climate and the fine harbors there, especially at Monterey. The Spanish claimed much of the area by right of discovery, but neither they, nor anyone else, did much to exploit California as the 1500s and the 1600s came and passed.

But they had an effect, nonetheless. As had happened everywhere in the New World, the Indians fell victim to new diseases brought in by the Europeans, like smallpox and the plague. By 1821 the Indian population of California had dropped to 200,000 from 300,000, which it had been only fifty years earlier.

Why was this salubrious land neglected by the Europeans, who had by 1700 settled the East Coast of North America all the way west to the Allegheny Mountains, the Caribbean Islands, huge areas of Central and South America, and had a thousand miles to the south developed a rich Hispanic culture in Mexico? It was mainly because they were too busy with these other settlements, and with developing trade in places like China, India, and the Pacific Islands. European interest in the New World almost always began as a search for something valuable to trade for, like the beaver skins of Canada, silk from China, spices from the Pacific Islands. California did not appear to have the kind of riches that would cause men to risk their lives and their fortunes to dig out. This is important to keep in mind: As we have seen in the case of Texas, it is usually the people who *settle* a land, not the adventurers and explorers looking for trade, who in the end truly possess it.

By the end of the 1600s the Spanish realized that they had better establish themselves in California if they expected to hang onto it. In 1697 the government encouraged the Roman Catholic order of Jesuits to build missions in Baja, California, eventually completing seventeen of them. The Jesuits' goal was to convert the Indians to Christianity, but the

Central to control of the California territory were the famous Spanish missions. As this etching of a mission at Santa Barbara, established in 1786, shows, missions were really small villages. The church at right is joined to quarters for the padres. Fields and pastures surround the mission building.

A recent photograph of a mission church at Alcala, near San Diego. The building has been partially restored. Note the bells, which regulated the life of the mission.

Spanish government saw the missions as a start on building a Spanish culture in California similar to the one that had existed for almost two centuries in Mexico.

Still, the decades rolled by, and only beginning in 1769 did the Spanish really start to settle the area that is now the state of California. In that year, with government support, another order of the Catholic Church, the Franciscans, began to build missions in California in order to convert the Indians. Twenty-one Franciscan missions were established between 1769 and 1823.

These missions have become famous in the lore of California. They were not simple churches, but small, self-sufficient communities. At the center was the mission building itself, usually designed as a rectangle surrounding an open courtyard. Here was the church, room for the *padres* (fathers) who ran the mission and shops. To one side were quarters for a small contingent of soldiers who protected the mission; to the other side houses for Indian laborers who did the bulk of the work. There would be extensive gardens, an orchard, a dam, a reservoir, and an irrigation system for the gardens, and large areas of pasture where grazed horses, cattle, and sheep. There were also on the missions workshops for making pottery, tanning hides, and blacksmithing. Some of these missions also owned *estancias*, or ranches, in outlying areas where more livestock was bred and raised.

To support the twenty-one Franciscan missions scattered through California, the Spanish established four *presidios*, or forts, manned by a few dozen soldiers. The presidios, too, had their own gardens and livestock, worked by Indian labor.

The most astonishing part of this story was the ability of the Spanish missionaries and the soldiers at the presidios to control the vastly larger number of Indians they had settled among. At the peak of the mission period about 1800, there were only around three thousand Hispanics (both officers and padres sent from Spain, and mixed-blood mestizos from Mexico) keeping more than twenty thousand Indians in peonage. How could this happen?

The answer is complicated. Religious groups at first felt that Indians should not be converted by force, and did not want to bring soldiers with them to the Indians. But after some missionaries had been killed, they saw the necessity of it. Still, they did not approve of forcible conversion. However, once an Indian had converted, the Spanish believed they had the right and duty to use force to keep the Indian in the mission, where he could attend mass regularly, and not, incidentally, work in the fields and the pastures. Indians who tried to run away from the missions were tracked down and whipped by the soldiers, and eventually they learned to do as they were told.

But why would the Indians convert to Christianity in the first place? Some may have been convinced of the superiority of the Christian religion; others may have wanted European clothes and the abundant food

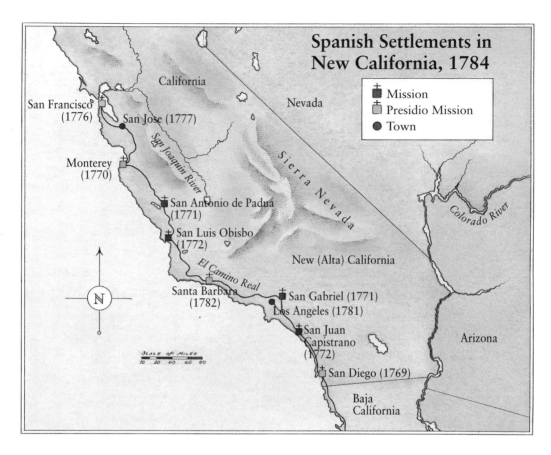

Spanish Settlements in
New California, 1784

California

San Francisco (1776)

San Jose (1777)

Nevada

San Joaquin River

Monterey (1770)

San Antonio de Padua (1771)

San Luis Obisbo (1772)

Sierra Nevada

New (Alta) California

Colorado River

El Camino Real

Santa Barbara (1782)

San Gabriel (1771)

Los Angeles (1781)

San Juan Capistrano (1772)

Arizona

San Diego (1769)

Baja California

N

SCALE OF MILES
10 20 40 60 80

	Mission
	Presidio Mission
	Town

the missions raised. But according to one historian, the power of the Spanish, with their armor, muskets, and cannon, had broken the "will of the Indian communities to offer further resistance to missionaries accompanied by soldiers." Individual Indians, of course, continued to run away whenever conditions became intolerable.

Worked by Indians for little or no pay, the missions became wealthy, mostly on the profits—especially in the international trade developed after Mexican independence—from raising livestock for the leather that came from cattle, sheep, pigs, goats, and horses. By the end of the 1700s the missions had four hundred thousand cattle, sixty thousand horses, three hundred thousand sheep and swine. The period of the missions—

about twenty years on each side of 1800—seemed to some people looking back on it as a kind of golden age. California's Governor Diego de Borica, in office from 1794 to 1800, wrote that in his land was a "climate healthful . . . plenty to eat . . . the most peaceful and quiet country in the world." Perhaps the Indians would not have agreed with this assessment.

But California could not be kept a secret forever. By the second half of the 1700s great chunks of the New World had been settled by Europeans. Transatlantic crossings were routine. Europeans had explored and in many cases taken control of portions of Asia. The western part of what would soon be the United States was one of the few areas of the world where Europeans had not made substantial inroads. Now they turned to it as one of the last areas open to exploitation.

In the Northwest, the major draw was beaver skins. The British, moving westward through Canada, began establishing trading posts in what is now British Columbia and the American Northwest. The Russians, who had claimed Alaska, not far from its Siberian territory, were working their way southward into the San Francisco area, also in search of beaver pelts. Beginning in 1786 a few adventurers from France and England made landings at the Spanish settlements at San Diego, Monterey, and San Francisco. In 1796 an American fur trader put in at Monterey. Very quickly other American ship captains, especially from New England, began to trade up and down the California coast. In 1801 these "Bostons," as the Californios called them, took eighteen thousand skins from California. Generally they would carry them to China, trade them for Chinese silks, tea, chinaware, and proceed to Europe, where they could sell the Chinese goods for enormous profits. Later, after Mexican independence in 1821, a huge trade in cowhides and tallow (animal fat) developed: The cowhides went to Boston for shoes, and the tallow went to Chile to make candles for miners. Sailors from these ships spread the word about the glories of the California climate and lush land. One celebrated book, published in 1840, Richard Henry Dana's *Two*

Years Before the Mast, gave Americans a glowing idea of the West Coast.

Authorities—under Spain until 1821 and then under Mexico—were perfectly happy to see trade develop in California, but they were reluctant to allow foreigners to settle there, knowing that their tiny Hispanic settlements could be swept aside by a flood of newcomers. Nonetheless, after 1800 a small number of foreigners managed to settle in California, mainly working as traders.

Thus matters stood in 1821 when Mexico broke away from Spain and established itself as an independent nation. Now California was Mexican; but as we have seen, governments in Mexico were tumbling over each other at a rapid pace, and it was difficult for the Mexicans to put together a coherent policy for the borderlands, including California. The missions had been making profits trading hides and tallow, at times illegally. Now Mexico legalized trade. Mexican merchants and investors salivated at the profits being made by the missions. In addition, Californios lusted for the mission lands. Together these groups pressured the government to take over the missions. In 1833 the Mexican government did so, and handed out huge areas the size of whole counties to Mexicans, most of them the Californios already living in California. The theory was that these lands would be settled by Mexicans, but while these huge ranches, worked by Indians as ever, made a handful of people extremely wealthy, they were not opened up to settlement by ordinary Mexicans.

By this time Americans were finally well aware of the very desirable country lying along the Pacific Coast of the continent. One problem with it was that to get there you had to cross the vast Great Plains filled with hostile Indians, and then the craggy Rocky Mountains, at places three hundred miles wide. A second problem was that, as we have seen, legitimate American claims to California were virtually nonexistent.

The area where American claims could best be supported was the so-called Oregon Territory, made up of what is today Oregon, Washington,

This was the way the Great Plains looked when the overlanders were first crossing it. The view is from the Platte River, which overlanders followed for part of the trek, about fifty miles from the base of the Rocky Mountains in the distance. It was a land filled with buffalo and other game, traversed by Indians; much of the time it was empty of human beings.

Idaho, parts of Montana, and parts of British Columbia at the western end of Canada. England, with its trading posts there, claimed this territory as well. Nonetheless, reports of potentially fine farmland, especially along the Columbia and Willamette Rivers, excited interest back east, and during the 1830s a few eager American pioneers made the long and dangerous trek out to Oregon and settled there. They showed that the trip, however difficult, could be made. In 1843 a huge party of a thousand people, traveling in covered wagons from St. Louis, made their way out to Fort Vancouver on the Columbia River. "Oregon Fever" swept the United States; some Americans began to make extravagant claims to territory all the way up to the line at 54°40' degrees of latitude, the bottom tip of the Russian claim—a line that lies some five hundred miles into present-day Canada. So passionate were American claims to this land that during the election of 1844 the slogan "fifty-four forty or fight" rang in the air.

Fortunately, neither the newly elected James Polk nor the majority of Congress were eager to tangle with Great Britain. Among other things, it was clear that the United States was soon likely to have a war with Mexico to fight. The majority of Americans came around to the idea that it was better to compromise than fight.

As it happened, a new government in England felt the same way. In 1844 the British Foreign Secretary, Lord Aberdeen, suggested a compromise plan, and on June 15, 1846, the Oregon Treaty was signed. It simply extended the old Canadian-American border along the 49th parallel to Puget Sound, and then through the Straits of Juan de Fuca to the Pacific. The British kept all of Vancouver Island, the tip of which jogs down below the 49th parallel, and navigation rights to the Columbia River.

The Oregon Treaty gave the United States an internationally accepted place on the Pacific Ocean. The nation now did stretch from sea to shining sea. The treaty was an example of how nations can deal reasonably with complex questions and work them out for the good of everybody without bloodshed, which, as we have seen, regrettably did not happen with Mexico.

Thus matters stood in 1848 when the Treaty of Guadalupe Hidalgo, ceding California to the United States, was signed. A few Americans had established themselves in California, some of whom had acquired huge ranches from the Mexican government and were growing wealthy. They were becoming a force in the still thinly settled land. The most important of the settlers, however, was a Swiss, John Augustus Sutter. He was a charismatic figure, intelligent and willing to use doubtful tactics to gain his ends. He built an establishment in the San Joaquin Valley that was really a small fort, with eighteen-foot walls protected by cannons. Inside Sutter's Fort was a small village of mills, shops, and homes, along with room for a thousand people. Sutter ruled over his establishment like a king.

By the end of the Mexican War, then, there were a considerable number of Americans and Europeans in California—traders, trappers, ranchers, ex-sailors looking for ways to make their fortunes. The Americans had an advantage over the rest, for they were aggressive, and there were millions of them back east hungering for land. By contrast, the wealthy Mexican *rancheros* had become accustomed to a slower-paced life. Their

This sketch of Sutter's Mill, where gold was first discovered in California, was published not long after the gold find. It shows the great interest in California that suddenly swept the settled parts of the United States.

wealth, built on land given to them for almost nothing and worked by badly paid Indians, had come too easy. But many of their daughters had married American merchants, and the line between Californios and Americans was not always clear. In any case, the old Californio families soon found themselves displaced by the aggressive newcomers. The Americans and Europeans like Sutter found room for themselves at the top. Then, in 1848, only months after the Treaty of Guadalupe Hidalgo was signed, some of Sutter's workmen found some glittering flecks of metal in a stream on Sutter's land. Sutter tried to keep the discovery of gold secret, for he knew it would bring a stampede of people; but word leaked out. After lingering for centuries in the twilight, California was suddenly a star in everybody's eyes.

CHAPTER VI

California Compromise

The California gold rush, which began in 1848 and peaked the next year, is one of the most dramatic events in American history. The stories of the pioneers in their covered wagons crossing two thousand miles of prairie through territory inhabited only by potentially hostile Indians and then heaving their wagons over the mountains have become a great American legend. In fact, the rush for gold itself, dominate as it did for a decade or so, probably had less effect on the later history of California than the legends have made it seem.

Despite efforts by Sutter to keep the discovery of gold quiet, by September 1848 the news had reached the East. In December President Polk reported the gold strike to Congress, and the rush was on. The expectations of the gold-seekers were unrealistic: Too many of them thought that chunks of gold were lying in stream bottoms waiting to be picked up. But the government did not discourage them, for its policy was to encourage Americans to settle the vast lands acquired in the Mexican War before others, especially the English, could challenge American rights in the West.

Earlier pioneers, especially those headed for Oregon, had worked out the system of crossing the plains and mountains that the gold seekers of 1849—the famous "forty-niners"—followed. They would gather at a jumping-off point on the Mississippi, usually St. Joseph or Independence, Missouri, in the spring, in order to get to the mountains and cross them before the snows fell. However, they could not leave until the prairie grass was mature enough to make fodder for their oxen and pack animals. In St. Joseph or other towns on the Mississippi they would pick up supplies and form into wagon trains, sometimes with as many as a hundred wagons—the slim canvas-covered wagons drawn by mules, horses, or oxen that came to be called prairie schooners.

Most of the overlanders were men, usually young men, but among them were a few families including women and children. They set off along the Mississippi, and thence northwest along the Platte River. This part of the trip was the easiest, but it was no picnic. Cholera and other diseases killed thousands. Others drowned crossing swollen rivers, and a good many, mostly farmers inexperienced with guns, accidentally shot themselves. After the Platte and North Platte, and a stop a Fort Laramie, travelers had to climb over the South Pass through the Rockies, cross the desert of the Great Basin, where human graves and animals dead of thirst lined the route, and finally make their tortuous way through high passes in the Sierra Nevada Mountains. Wagons had to be shoved and hauled up incredibly steep inclines, and then sometimes lowered inch by inch down the equally steep paths on the other side. Some got caught in the snows, like the famous Donner party, who were stranded in the mountains in 1847 by a blizzard and ended up eating the bodies of their dead to keep alive.

There was an alternate route that ran south around the bottom end of the Rockies, across the desert lands of New Mexico into San Diego. But this took you through Death Valley, with its "dreadful sands and shadows . . . salt columns, bitter lakes and wild, dreary desolation." Several thousand gold seekers also traveled a southern route across Texas

These cartoons mock the tens of thousands of people who rushed to California after gold. At left, gold-seekers attempt to board ships at the Isthmus of Panama. These ships were often overcrowded and passage was difficult to obtain. At right, gold miners, burdened with sacks of gold, attempt to buy passage home. In fact, most of the gold-seekers got little or nothing for their pains.

to El Paso, Tucson, and Yuma to San Diego and then up to the goldfields. A substantial number of gold-seekers went by ship to California, either around the Horn, or to the Isthmus of Panama and across to the Pacific, where they hoped to find another ship. But it was the overland trek, whether for settlement or gold, that captured the imagination of America.

One important group of overlanders was the Mormons. This religious group was formed in the 1820s by a young visionary, Joseph Smith. He slowly gathered adherents, and through the next decades made a series of moves, frequently driven out by neighboring people who disliked his unorthodox ideas about religion and society. Smith was murdered in 1844, and his followers concluded that they would never have peace in the United States. Under Brigham Young, a smart, tough man with great leadership abilities, groups of Mormons began the arduous trip west, looking for an isolated place where they could build a home safe from persecution.

The Mormons found a place for themselves in the valley of the Great Salt Lake among the Wasatch Mountains, and here, in the summer of 1847 they began to build a new community. As with other pioneers, there was much suffering and hardship, but the little community held on, and grew, fed by immigrants coming not only from the eastern United States, but from Europe as well. Using precious water flowing in streams from the mountains, the Mormons established a rigidly controlled irrigation system that allowed farms to sprout in the desert. The California gold rush of 1849 was a bonanza to the Mormons, for they were able to sell food, mules, and horses to the overlanders at exorbitant prices. Others of them charged three dollars a day, then an exorbitant wage, for repairing overlanders' wagons. By the 1850s the Mormon community of the Latter-Day Saints, as it is still called, was flourishing.

However, most of the overlanders did not go west for religious reasons, but for gold. They quickly discovered that it was not lying in

The Mormon leader Brigham Young was not just a visionary but a clever and dynamic man who knew how to deal with practical matters, like land development and water rights.

chunks, but had to be worked out of the ground painfully. Most panned for gold in streams. Filling a shallow pan with mud and pebbles, they would slosh it around until the mud washed away hoping to glean a few grains of gold dust that would have sunk to the bottom of the pan. In many cases men banded together to wash their gold in a cradle, or rocker, a rough device of timber set up near a stream in which a larger amount of dirt could be panned at a time. Others dug into mountainsides hoping to find veins of purer gold. Whatever the method, it was hard, time-consuming, and often futile. Then, many of those who found gold spent it foolishly in the many saloons and gambling halls that had sprung up to take advantage of the miners.

Nonetheless, huge amounts of gold did flow into rapidly growing cities like Sacramento and San Francisco. These towns boomed. Rough wooden buildings were thrown up to house stores, theaters, saloons, and warehouses. Almost anything could be sold for exorbitant prices, and

One of the most common systems of collecting gold was by panning it. The miner filled his pan with mud and pebbles from a stream bottom and sloshed water around in it, tipping it this way and that to sluice the dirt out. Gold, being heavier, would sink to the bottom. Sometimes two or more miners worked together with a homemade rocker, like the one shown in this picture. This system was somewhat more efficient, but still, most of the miners got small rewards for much work.

many people got rich, not from digging gold, but from selling to the miners picks, tent canvas, food, and bedding.

One of the greatest problems facing the immigrants was the lack of any kind of civil government in 1849 and 1850. California was theoretically run by a military government. The military force was too small to control effectively the tens of thousands of new people pouring in. In some instances the old Mexican authorities remained in power. But in many cases miners in the rough mining camps, often just towns of tents centered on a few wooden stores and gambling halls, formed their own governments, elected their own mayors and judges, held their own trials, and hanged robbers and murderers themselves.

But this rough justice was no substitute for real law and order. The new Californians were eager for admission as a state; and so were people gathering in the Southwest, the Oregon Territory, on the Great Plains, and elsewhere. And inevitably, the old, explosive issue of slavery cropped up. Would any new states be slave or free?

This sketch from a contemporary magazine shows a rough California mining town. Note that some of the buildings, like the "Clubhouse" and the "Sunnyside Hotel," are made of canvas stretched over wooden frames.

We need to look back to February 1818, when the House of Representatives began to consider the admission of Missouri, the first of the states to be carved out of the huge Louisiana Purchase lands. In Missouri slaves amounted to a sixth of the population. The debates in Congress over Missouri were violent and angry. The more populous North had the majority in the House of Representatives and passed a bill that would gradually eliminate slavery in Missouri. The Senate, where

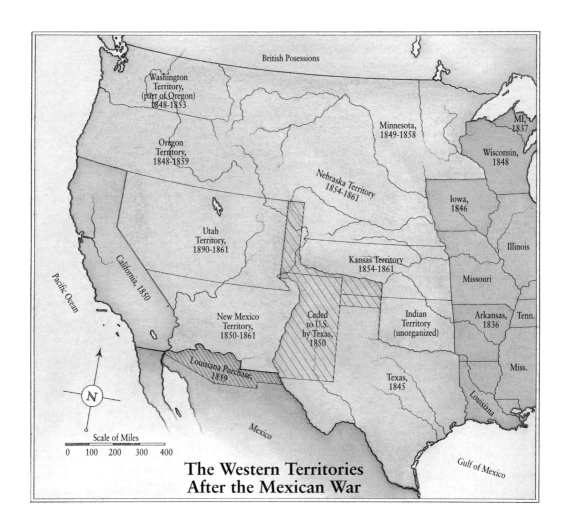

The Western Territories
After the Mexican War

the South had greater strength, passed a bill admitting Missouri with no limits at all on slavery. The Congress was thus deadlocked, and Southerners were beginning to talk about splitting off from the Union if they did not get their way in Missouri. The idea of the nation breaking into two pieces appalled many patriots. (This story is told in the volume in this series called *Slavery and the Coming of the Civil War*.) The great statesman Henry Clay worked hard with others determined to keep the

Union together to find a compromise. Finally he worked out a deal. Maine, which was also up for statehood, would come in as a free state, Missouri as a slave state. A line would be drawn at the southern border of Missouri through the rest of the Louisiana Purchase (latitude 36°30'): New states—except Missouri—north of that line would be free, ones south of it would be slave.

The uproar over the admission of Missouri in 1820 awakened the issue a lot of Americans had hoped they could duck. Northerners saw the Missouri Compromise as a victory for the South, and they grew more determined that next time they would not give in, but keep slavery out of new territory completely. The South grew equally determined that slavery would not be tampered with: Slaves were property and must be protected by law like any other property.

Nonetheless, for a generation the Missouri Compromise kept the conflict in check. But now, with potential statehood for Oregon, California, and New Mexico looming, the hard divisive issue was raised again.

The intense feelings raised by the slavery issue had a number of causes. In general, Southerners believed that they had to have slaves to work the sugar, cotton, and tobacco fields. They also hated the idea of having blacks raised up to the level of whites as free citizens. Perhaps most important, they were determined not to let the North, with its rapidly growing population and powerful industrial machinery, push them around.

In the North, many people believed that slavery was immoral and unchristian, and ought to be stopped. Heating up this feeling were the writings of radical abolitionists who wanted to end slavery everywhere immediately. They convinced many Northerners that slavery and Christianity were irreconcilable. But attitudes were more complicated than that. Many other Northerners thought that even though slavery was wrong, blacks were naturally inferior, incapable of learning, and would always have menial jobs, free or slave. Northerners who were pouring into the Oregon Territory, California, and Utah carried these attitudes with them. They did not want slavery in their territories, because they did not want blacks there at all. Gold miners, for example, did not want to compete with slave labor for jobs, and many felt it would be degrading to work side by side with a black. Not all of the immigrants were so strongly antiblack; some were willing to accept African Americans as fellow citizens. But the majority were opposed to them. And they were determined to keep slavery out of the new territories.

The battle boiled to a head in the Senate in the early months of 1850. It resulted in some of the finest debates and greatest speechmaking ever in the American Congress. The first up was Henry Clay. Some thirty years earlier he had pushed through the Missouri Compromise, which had held the Union together. Now aging, he was determined to do it again. He offered a complex compromise that would admit California as a free state, but would put no restrictions on slavery in the rest of the land acquired from Mexico. The United States government would take over the large debts owed

The Compromise of 1850 was initially worked out by the Kentucky statesman Henry Clay. It was eventually passed a bit at a time after much battling in Congress.

by the formerly independent nation of Texas. Slave trading would be ended in the District of Columbia, people helping slaves to run away would be severely punished, and Congress would resolve that it had no authority to end the selling of slaves across state borders. Clay's compromise was thus a grab bag, with something for the North balanced off against something for the South.

Clay's compromise was answered by the once-powerful John Calhoun, who was now so ill that somebody else had to read his speech for him. He insisted that the North had pushed the South around enough, and a line had to be drawn in the dirt: All new territory had to be open to slavery. Otherwise, the South must secede from the Union, and fight the North if it had to.

On March 7, the great orator Daniel Webster responded to Calhoun with one of the greatest speeches ever made in Congress. He began, "I speak today for the preservation of the Union. Hear me for my cause," and concluded, "There can be no peaceable secession," and begged his fellow Northerners to compromise and show a friendly spirit toward the South. Webster's speech was reprinted in newspapers around the country and was much applauded, but it did not change the minds of many senators. The Congress was gradually brought around to what is now called the Compromise of 1850 simply because there was no other choice. The new territories contained vast acres of fertile soil, several fine ports, rapidly growing cities and towns, and all that California gold. There was a lot of money to be made not merely by the overlanders rolling westward, but by Eastern merchants, shippers, growers, and countless other entrepreneurs. Beyond this, if the new territories were not taken under the American flag, they might in desperation turn to other nations for protection.

President Zachary Taylor, a Southerner, was opposed to the compromise, but in July he died suddenly, and his vice president, Millard Fillmore, took over. Fillmore was eager for the compromise and finally,

One of the most famous speeches ever given in Congress was made by Daniel Webster, when he urged Americans to support the Compromise of 1850. The speech, eloquent as it was, probably did not change many minds, and the compromise was passed by heavy politicking.

in September, it went through Congress. Its terms were these: California would come in as a free state. The eventual settlers in the rest of the territory gained from Mexico would be allowed to decide the question of slavery for themselves until the territories became states, when, of course, like any state they could vote slavery up or down. This was the so-called "popular sovereignty" provision. The Fugitive Slave Law, which required government officials everywhere to assist in the capture of runaway slaves, was tightened with legal arrangements highly favorable to slave owners and stacked heavily against blacks; the slave trade was forbidden in Washington, D.C.; and a few smaller matters were settled.

Most Americans were vastly relieved that the explosive issue had been defused before it could destroy the United States. Probably the majority of Americans believed that finally the slavery question had been settled for good. And yet eleven years later, the nation would explode in a terrible Civil War.

But a least a way was open for the new lands to be brought in as states. Eventually they would be admitted as New Mexico, Arizona, California, Utah, Nevada, Washington, Oregon, and Idaho. The United States now straddled the continent, and the new lands would add much to the strength and prosperity of the nation. Manifest destiny had been achieved.

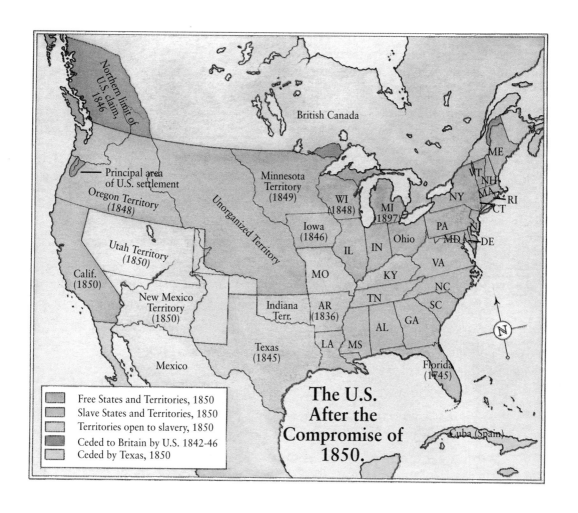

The U.S. After the Compromise of 1850.

Free States and Territories, 1850
Slave States and Territories, 1850
Territories open to slavery, 1850
Ceded to Britain by U.S. 1842-46
Ceded by Texas, 1850

BIBLIOGRAPHY

Many of the books that are out of print may be found in school or public libraries.

For Students

Blumberg, Rhoda. *The Great American Gold Rush*. New York: Bradbury Press, 1989.

Carter, Alden R. *Last Stand at the Alamo*. New York: Franklin Watts, 1990.

Fisher, Leonard Everett. *The Alamo*. New York: Holiday House, 1987.

___. *The Oregon Trail*. New York: Holiday House, 1990.

Hoobler, Dorothy and Thomas. *The Mexican American Family Album*. New York: Oxford University Press, 1994.

Jones, Mary Ellen. *The American Frontier*: Opposing Viewpoints. San Diego, CA: Greenhaven Press, 1994.

O'Brien, Steven. *Antonio Lopez de Santa Anna.* Hispanics of Achievement Series. New York: Chelsea House, 1992.

Ryan, Bryan, and Nicolas Kanellos, eds. *Hispanic American Almanac.* Detroit: Gale Research, UXL, 1995.

Smith, Carter, ed. *The Conquest of the West: A Sourcebook on the American West.* Brookfield, CT: Millbrook Press, 1992.

For Teachers

Bauer, K. Jack. *The Mexican War, 1846–1848.* New York: Macmillan, 1974. Reprint. Lincoln: University of Nebraska Press, 1995.

Billington, Ray Allen. *The Far Western Frontier, 1830–1860.* 4th ed. New York: Macmillan, 1974. Reprint. Albuquerque: University of New Mexico Press, 1995.

Binkley, William. *Texas Revolution.* Baton Rouge: Louisiana State University Press, 1952. Reprint. Austin: Texas State Historical Association, 1979.

Brandon, *William. Quivira: Europeans in the Region of the Santa Fe Trail, 1540–1820.* Athens: Ohio University Press, 1990.

Harlow, Neal. *California Conquered: War and Peace on the Pacific, 1846–1850,* 1982. Reprint. Berkeley and Los Angeles: University of California Press, 1989.

Holt, Michael F. *The Political Crisis of the 1850's.* New York: John Wiley, 1978. Reprint. New York: W.W. Norton, 1983.

Horsman, Reginald. *Race and Manifest Destiny: The Origins of American Racial Anglo-Saxonism*, 1981. Cambridge: Harvard University Press, 1986.

Lamar, Howard. *The Far Southwest, 1846–1912.* New Haven: Yale University Press, 1970.

Limerick, Patricia Nelson. *Legacy of Conquest: The Unbroken Past of the American West.* New York: W.W. Norton, 1987.

Merk, Frederick. *History of the Western Movement.* New York: Alfred A. Knopf, 1978.

___. *The Monroe Doctrine and American Expansion, 1843–1849.* New York: Alfred A. Knopf, 1966.

Meyer, Michael C., and William L. Sherman. *The Course of Mexican History.* 5th ed. New York: Oxford University Press, 1995.

Morison, Samuel Eliot. *The European Discovery of America: The Southern Voyages.* New York: Oxford University Press, 1974.

Simmons, Marc. *Last Conquistador: Juan de Onate and the Settling of the Far Southwest.* Norman: University of Oklahoma Press, 1991.

Stegmaier, Mark J. Texas, *New Mexico and the Compromise of 1850: Boundary Dispute and Sectional Crisis*, 1970. Kent, OH: Kent State University Press, 1996.

Unruh, John D., Jr. *The Plains Across: The Overland Emigrants and the Trans-Mississippi West, 1840–1860*, 1979. Urbana: University of Illinois Press, 1993.

Weber, David J., ed. *Foreigners in Their Native Lands: Historical Roots of the Mexican Americans*. Albuquerque: University of New Mexico Press, 1973.

___. *The Spanish Frontier in North America*. Yale Western Americana Series. New Haven: Yale University Press, 1992.

List of Maps
Mexican War, **55**
National Territorial Claims in Western North
     America, **43**
Oregon Boundary, **36**
Routes to the West, **79**
Spanish Explorers in the American South, **10**
Spanish Settlements in New California, 1784,
     64
The U.S. After the Compromise of 1850, **84**
The Western Territories After the Mexican
     War, **78**

adobe, 27
adventure, 39
African Americans, 26, 27, 80–81
agriculture, 14, 25
The Alamo, **30**, 33
Alaska, 34
Albuquerque, 42
Apache Indians, 17, 20, 24
Arizona, 9, 16–17, 56
Austin, Moses, 31
Austin, Stephen, 31
Aztec Indians, 10–11, **11**, **12**, 57

Baja California, 60, 61. *See also* California
basketry, 14, 59, **59**
blacks, 26, 27, 80–81
Bonaparte, Napoléon, 29
Borica, Governor Diego de, 65
Boston, 65
"Bostons," 65
Bowie, William B., 33
bribery, 28, 51
British Columbia, 65, 67
Brownsville, Texas, 50
bubonic plague, 13, 60
Buena Vista, Mexico, 51
buffalo, 14
buildings, **25**, 27

calendars, Pueblo, 21
Calhoun, John, 82
California
     golden age of, 64–65
     gold rush, 55–56, 71–76, **73**, **76**, 77
     Hispanic population of, 28, 42, 51
     Indians living in, 58–60, **59**, 62–65
     Mexican control of, 34, 42
     routes to, 71–74

California *(Continued)*
  Russian claims on, 34
  Spanish missions in, 61–62, 66
  statehood, 76–77
  trade activity in, 65–66
Californios, 51, 66, 69–70
Canada, 65, 67–68
Caribbean Islands, 10
Catholic Church, 16, 28, 63–64. *See also*
  missionary activity; missions
cattle, 31, 44, 64. *See also* cowhides
Central America, 10
Chapultepec castle, 53–54, **54**
children, Indian, 25
Chile, 65
China, 56, 65
Christianity. *See also* missionary activity;
  missions
  views on slavery, 80
Churubusco, Mexico, 52–53
Ciudad Juàrez, Mexico, 21, 23
classes, social, 27–28
Clay, Henry, 79–80, **81**, 81–82
clothing, 24, 25, 63–64
Colorado, 34
Columbia River, 67–68
Columbus, Christopher, 10
Comanche Indians, 24
Compromise of 1850, 81–82
conquest, wars of, 57
conquistadores, 60
Coronado, Francisco Vàsquez de, 16
corruption, 28
Cortez, Hernando, 10–11, **14**, **15**
cotton, 31, 38, 80
cowhides, 65
criollos, 40
Crockett, Davy, **30**, 33
culture
  black, 26, 27
  of California Indians, 60

English, 24
Hispanic, 24–25
Indian, 14, 25, **26**, 26–27

Dana, Richard Henry, 65–66
Death Valley, 72
descent, pure Spanish *vs* mixed, 26–27
diet, 14, 24–25, 27, 58, 63–64
diseases, 13, 60
Donner party, 72
do Soto, Hernando, 18
dwellings
  of California Indians, 59
  construction materials, 27
  of Plains Indians, 14
  of Pueblo Indians, 14–15

1850, Compromise of, 81–82
El Paso, 21, 23, 25, 28
England
  interest in northwest territory, 40, 65, 67
  interest in Texas, 47
  settlers from, 9, 10, 17, 24
españoles, 26, 40
explorers, vs settlers, 17, 57, 61

farmland, 29–31
"fifty-four forty or fight," 67–68
Fillmore, President Millard, 82–83
fishing, 17, 38
food, 14, 24–25, 27, 58, 63–64
Fort Laramie, Wyoming, **41**, 72
forts, 42, 63, 69
forty-niners, 71–74
Foster, Kan, **37**
Franciscan missionaries
  in California, 62
  in New Mexico, 16–17
  in opposition to governors, 19
  and spread of Hispanic culture, 24–25
French, in North America, 10, 19, 65

French Revolution, 29
frontier, 9, 27, 29–31
The Fugitive Slave Law, 83
fur trade, 19, 34, 58, 61, 65

Gadsden, James, 56
Gadsden Purchase, 56
Germans, 9
Gila River, 56
Gil Ybarbo, Antonio, 27
goats, 64
gold rush, 55–56, 71–76, **73, 76, 77**
governors
    españoles as, 27–28
    opposition to Franciscan missionaries, 19
Great Salt Lake, 74
Guadalupe Hidalgo, Treaty of, 54–55, 68
guns, 16

Haiti, 29
harbors, 38
Hispanic culture, 24–28
Hopi Indians, 15, 20, 23
horses, 13–14, **18,** 64
Houston, Sam, **32,** 33, 45
human sacrifice, **12**
hunting, 58–59

Idaho, 34, 84
Independence, Missouri, 72
India, 60–61
Indians. *See also specific Indian peoples*
    in California, 58–60, **59**
    enmity among, 20
    and European diseases, 13, 60
    and horses, 13–14
    and manifest destiny, 39
    relations with Spaniards, 16–27
    women and children, 25
intermarriage, 25–26
Irish settlers, 9

Iroquois Indians, 59

Jackson, President Andrew, 45, 48
Jamestown, Virginia, 9
Jefferson, President Thomas, 31
Jemez, New Mexico, 20, **25**
Jesuit missionaries, 61–62
jet, 14
jewelry, 14

kachina masks, 20
kivas, 20

labor, forced, 19, 43. *See also* peonage;
    slavery
land, 38–39, 42–44
language, 24–25, 32
Louisiana, 19
Louisiana Purchase, 31

Maine, 80
Malinalco, Temple at, **11**
manifest destiny, 37–44, 46–47, 56–57
marriage, 25–26
masks, 20
measles, 13
Mesilla Valley, 56
mestizos, 25–26, 41
Mexican War
    attitude of Americans toward, **50,** 50–51
    battles, 51–54
    cartoons about, **46**
    consequences of, 55–56
    historians' attitude toward, 45
    as moral issue, 56–57
    photograph of, **52**
    poster for, **50**
    and statehood for Texas, 48–49
    Treaty of Guadalupe Hidalgo, 54–55, 68
Mexico, 10–11, 26, 27. *See also* Mexican
    War

Mexico *(Continued)*
  Americans view of, 42–44
  attitude toward America, 56
  attitude toward borderlands, 41–42, 43–44
  and cowhide trade, 65
  economic conditions in, 28
  independence of, 29
  political conditions, 40–44, 49, 52, 56–57
  and trade development in California, 66
  university in, 40
Mexico City, 28, 32, 52–54
missionary activity, 16–20, 61–64
missions. *See also* Alamo
  in California, 43, **61**, 61–65, **62**, 66
  government takeover of, 66
  physical layout of, 62–63
  remains of, in New Mexico, **25**
  and spread of Hispanic culture, 19, 24–25
Mississippi River
  as eastern edge of Spanish territory, 18
  expansion west of the, 29–31, 35–37
Missouri Compromise, 78–83
Molina del Rey, Mexico, 53
Monterey, California, 65
Monterey, Mexico, 51
Mormons, 74
Moscoso, Luis de, 18
mountain men, **37**
mulatto, 27
musical instruments, Aztec, **12**

Napoléon Bonaparte, 29
Navajo Indians, 17, 20, 24, **26**
Nevada, 9, 84
New Mexico
  demographic data, 28, 42
  Indian rebellion in, 20–23
  precious metals and jewels in, 16–17
  purchase by U. S., 56
  on route to California, 72
  Texas' claims on, 48–49

Niños Héroes, 52–53
Niza, Fray Marcos de, 16
Nuestra Señora de la Conquista, 23

Oklahoma, 36
Oñate, Juan de, 17
Oregon, 34, 84
"Oregon Fever", 67
Oregon Territory, 66–67, 77
Oregon Treaty, 68
overlanders, **67**, 71–74

Pacific Islands, 61
Pacific Ocean, expansion to, 37–39
padres, 62
peonage, 63
pigs, 64
pioneers, **35**, 35–37, **37**, **40**, 67. *See also*
  overlanders
Plains Indians
  and horses, 13–14, 18
  relations with Pueblo Indians, 20–21
Platte River, **67**, 72
Plymouth, Massachusetts, 9
Polk, President James K., **48**, 48–51, 68
Popé, 21
"popular sovereignty," 83
population growth, 35
Portuguese, 10
pottery, 14
poverty, 19, 28, 41
presidios, 43, 63
priests, 62
Pueblo Indians
  allies of Spaniards, 23
  culture of, 14–17
  relations with Plains Indians, 20–21
  and Spanish missionaries, 19–20
pueblos, 23
Puritans, 39

racial mixing, 25–26
railway, 56
ranches, 42
rebellions. *See also* French Revolution
   by British colonies, 29
   in Haiti, 29
   by Indians, 20–24
   in Mexico, 29
   in Texas, 30, 32–33
Red River, 34
religion
   Aztec, 11, 12
   of California Indians, 60, 63–64
   Christian (see Catholic Church;
     missionary activity; missions)
   Mormon, 74
   Pueblo, 20
revolutions. *See* French Revolution;
   rebellions
Rio Grande, 21
Rivera, Diego
   Cortez's arrival at Vera Cruz painting, **15**
Rocky Mountains, 34
routes, transcontinental, **67**, 71–74
Russians, 34, 39–40, 44, 65, 67–68

Sacramento, California, 75
sacrifice, human, **12**
Salazar of Zacatecas, Antonio, 27
San Antonio, Texas, 33
San Diego, California, 65
San Francisco, California, 56, 65, 75
San Jacinto, 33
San Juan, Pueblo of, 21
Santa Anna, General Antonio López de, 29,
   41, 51–53, 56
Santa Fe, New Mexico, 17, 21, 23, 51
sarape, Navaho, **26**
schools, 32
Scott, General Winfield, 51
sea ports, 38

settlers, vs explorers, 17, 57, 61
Seven Cities of C'bolo, 16
sheep, 31, 44, 64
silk, 61, 65
silver, 16, 27
Sioux, 59
slavery
   differing views on, 80–81
   as statehood issue, 47–48, 77–80
slaves
   blacks, 25–26, 27
   Indian, 11, 25, 27, 43
Slidell, John, 49
smallpox, 13, 60
Smith, Joseph, 74
society, classes within, 27–28
South America, 10
Southwestern United States
   Hispanic influence in, 9–10
Spaniards. *See also españoles*
governing class, 27
relations with Indians, 16–26
in South and Central America, 10
in Southwestern United States, 9–10
in Spain, 28
territorial claims, 18
spices, 61
St. Joseph, Missouri, 72
sugar, 80
Sutter, John Augustus, 68–69
Sutter's Mill, **69**

tallow, 65
Taos, New Mexico, 20–21
taxes, 19
Taylor, Zachary, 50, **53**, 82
tea, 65
Tenochtitlàn, 10–11
Texas
   American settlement of, 31–32
   claims to New Mexico territory, 48–49

Texas *(Continued)*
  and cotton, 38
  Hispanic population of, 18–19, 28, 42
  independence of, 32–33, 56
  missionary activity in, 18–19
  on route to California, 72–74
  statehood for, 35, 45–48, 56
textiles, 38
timber, 17
tobacco, 17, 80
tools, 16, 25, 59, **59**
trade
  and bribery, 28
  and California Indians, 60
  cowhide, 65
  English, with Indians, 65
  fur, 19, 34, 58, 61, 65
  and manifest destiny, 38
  New Englanders, and California, 65
  silk, 61, 65
  spices, 61
  tallow, 65
  U.S. with Far East, 56, 60–61
trading posts, 40, 65
Travis, William B., 33
treaties
  Guadalupe Hidalgo, 54–55, 68
  Oregon, 68
Treaty of Guadalupe Hidalgo, 54–55, 68
turquoise, 14
Two Years Before the Mast, 66

University of Mexico, 40
upward mobility, 27
Utah, 9, 84
Ute Indians, 24

Van Buren, President Martin, 48
Vargas, Diego de, 23
Vásquez de Coronado, Francisco, 16
Vera Cruz, Mexico, **15**, 51–52

War, Mexican. *See* Mexican War
Washington, 34, 84
Washington D. C., 83
wealth, 28
Webster, John, 82, **83**
westward expansion, 9, 29–31, **35**, 35–39, **40**
whaling, 38, **38**
Willamette River, 67
women, Indian, 25
Wood, General Robert, **52**
writing, 16

Xipe Topec, **12**

Ybarbo, Lt. Antonio Gil, 27
Young, Brigham, 74, **75**

Zacatecas, Antonio Salazar of, 27
Zuñi Indians, 15, 20

JAMES LINCOLN COLLIER is the author of a number of books both for adults and for young people, including the social history *The Rise of Selfishness in America*. He is also noted for his biographies and historical studies in the field of jazz. Together with his brother, Christopher Collier, he has written a series of award-winning historical novels for children widely used in schools, including the Newbery Honor classic, *My Brother Sam Is Dead*. A graduate of Hamilton College, he lives with his wife in New York City.

CHRISTOPHER COLLIER grew up in Fairfield County, Connecticut and attended public schools there. He graduated from Clark University in Worcester, Massachusetts and earned M.A. and Ph.D. degrees at Columbia University in New York City. After service in the Army and teaching in secondary schools for several years, Mr. Collier began teaching college in 1961. He is now Professor of History at the University of Connecticut and Connecticut State Historian. Mr. Collier has published many scholarly and popular books and articles about Connecticut and American history. With his brother, James, he is the author of nine historical novels for young adults, the best known of which is *My Brother Sam Is Dead*. He lives with his wife Bonnie, a librarian, in Orange, Connecticut.